American Travels of a Dutch Hobo   1923 - 1926

American Travels of a Dutch Hobo

1923 - 1926

GERARD LEEFLANG

IOWA STATE UNIVERSITY PRESS / AMES

© 1984 The Iowa State University Press
All rights reserved

Composed by Typeco, Inc., Des Moines, Iowa 50309
Printed by The Iowa State University Press, Ames, Iowa 50010

First edition, 1984

Library of Congress Cataloging in Publication Data

Leeflang, Gerard, 1901–
    American travels of a Dutch hobo, 1923–1926.

    1. United States – Description and travel – 1920–1940. 2. United States – Social life and customs – 1918-1945. 3. Leeflang, Gerard, 1901-   . 4. Tramps – United States. 5. Dutch – United States. I. Title.
E169.L45   1984   973.91′5092′4   84–8975
ISBN 0–8138–0888–X

CONTENTS

PREFACE

THAT I, after so many years, troubled myself in trying to describe what I lived to see the years I spent in the United States of America more than half a century ago is mainly due to my yielding to the insistence of my American friends and, above all, of my granddaughters. As to these latter, they suffer from the same incurable disease as I did—and in a way still do—namely, waywardness of mind, craving to go where new aspects of life loom up from behind the horizons, to walk unknown paths, not the way though as I did in my youthful impetuousness. It is because of their pressure that I felt obliged to lay down my experiences of that long ago.

In order to underline or better to support my scribbling about the places where I lived and the situations I dropped into, I made a number of pen drawings, which in my humble opinion may add to enliven my narrative and perhaps make it more credible. For, I daresay, after so many years man's memory may play him false; should this become obvious then I beg the reader to show mercy. Illustrations like those printed herewith may contribute to stimulate thinking, which was the case with me when writing. Anyway, they will enable the reader to visualize the time of life in the U.S.A. half a century ago—the time when I happened to live as an alien between the concrete blocks of Manhattan, in the Corn Belt of the Middle West, and amidst the magnificent shopping centers and the liquor gangs of Chicago.

What was left of old photographs and sketches, kept in my drawers for years, rendered me a good turn in making my drawings when my memory was lacking. I, too, had a good many data at my disposal, received from my American friends in the course of time, and I also must give credit to the Chicago Public Library and the library of Cleveland, Ohio, for supplying me with some information, for which I do thank them as yet.

With a view to consider the feelings of those who may still be living, or if they don't, of their descendants with respect to some incidents mentioned, I changed the names of the persons concerned.

In conclusion, I have tried to open the door ajar to cast a glance on the Roaring Twenties as I saw them. If my story induces people to lose themselves in it, I shall be satisfied.

G.L.

INTRODUCTION

IN the summer of 1923 a young Dutch seaman arrived in New York City. Although he had traveled extensively in his job as radio operator, he had never visited the United States. The Statue of Liberty and Manhattan skyline had a special impact upon him. During his first days in port he visited many of the standard tourist attractions, saw Babe Ruth hit a home run at Yankee Stadium, ate at a hot dog stand, and toured Harlem, Central Park, and Chinatown. By the fourth day he had decided to jump ship since his fascination for Manhattan outweighed the risk of punishment for abandoning his duties as a seaman. Thus began Gerard Leeflang's American odyssey which lasted until his deportation to his homeland on September 30, 1926.

After almost sixty years of remembering and telling stories of his youthful adventures in America to his grandchildren, Gerard Leeflang, who pursued a journalistic career in his native land, wrote these reminiscences. For reasons which seem important to him, Leeflang distinguished between hoboes as respectable vagabonds and tramps as ne'er-do-wells. He saw himself, with some justification, as a Dutch hobo traveling in America.

The reminiscences contain numerous musings about social conditions in the various places Leeflang visited and lived in the United States, with some comments on the race and nationality of the people. As a young man just becoming acquainted with this country, he observed and criticized prejudice and discrimination, especially toward blacks, but revealed hints of those same attitudes towards Jews. He seems somewhat traditional in his attitudes toward women, rejecting the tendency of his companion Jörgen Dahl and many other men to want "the girls" for what appears to be sexual satisfaction while being struck by the degree of self-reliance or emancipation of some individual women he met.

Not surprising, because of his youth and background, Leeflang had little knowledge of the political processes of this nation. The lull in economic activity before the presidential election as business leaders waited to see who would win and what policies would be followed, seemed revealing to him.

Leeflang's descriptions of the cities he visited are somewhat routine to one familiar with their histories, but also are quite accurate. In fact, there is some authenticity to the reminiscences since he makes no effort to provide precise facts which could be easily established by simple research, such as checking any standard source to eliminate the statement that Warren Harding "might have had to resign" because an investigation by a Senate committee revealed his guilt, but he died before the disgraceful revelations."

The Iowa years tell of farm and small-town life. Readers familiar with Carl Hamilton's *In No Time At All* will find variations of the themes of hard work, plowing, planting and picking corn, care of livestock including milking since both of Leeflang's employers had dairy herds, surgery to neuter male animals which were to be fattened for slaughter, horse and tractor farming, and adventures with Model T Fords.

Two features set Leeflang's experiences apart from Hamilton's reminiscences. Leeflang was a newcomer, a foreigner; and Leeflang records some of the social life of the community. As a newcomer and foreigner, but with readily apparent respectability and reliability, Leeflang cites his quick acceptance in the community and participation in community social events held in homes, at school, and other places. Leeflang particularly set himself against Jörgen Dahl who is described as unmannered, incompatible, and unrefined in his associations with women. Dahl eventually became known as a scofflaw who resorted to bootlegging.

In the Kelley, Iowa, area Leeflang noticed the diverse national origin of the people. That diversity did not seem to create excessive social tension, but, of course, those people were all of northern and western European stock, as was he. Since he mingled easily with the Kelley residents, he made no effort to seek out persons of Dutch nativity or heritage even though the 1920 census shows Iowa had the largest number of residents born in the Netherlands of any census year between 1850 and 1940.[1]

Leeflang did well in the United States. He spoke some English, which enabled him to deal effectively with Americans and get ahead of newly arrived immigrants who sought the same jobs he wanted. At the same time, he benefitted from his recent arrival from the old country since many people wanted to hear his accounts of life and conditions there. He quickly obtained employment; when useful he traded on his experience as a ship's radio operator to convince supervisors that he was capable of better jobs. While earning $50.00 per month as a farmhand he owned a horse and later he bought a car which enabled him to travel around central Iowa and as far as Nebraska. People in the Kelley area assumed that he would marry a farmer's daughter and settle there.

The reminiscenses add something to Iowa literature because there is a dearth of similar published material by foreign nationals who lived in the state in the early twentieth century. Leeflang's hobo wanderings provide contrasting urban and rural experiences and he seemed to do well in both settings. He was capable, he was versatile, he was eager and responsive to new experiences. For a short time, as he notes, Gerard Leeflang attained some of the American dream.

Leeflang gives some credit for research assistance to two libraries in the United States, and in many cases there is ground for believing that he could not precisely recall all the information he includes, yet much of the account of his life in the United States seems to be from memory. The story is one continuing narrative, which has been divided by the editor into chapters according to time and place. The editing has been minimal so that Leeflang's own form of expression in English is retained. That form of expression gives a special flavor to the work without being obscure or excessively disruptive to the narrative. The drawings, as the author notes, are recent efforts based upon old photographs and sketches he made during his youthful tour of the United States.

*　　*　　*

---

[1]U.S. Bureau of the Census, *16th Census*, vol. 2, pt. 2 (1940), 865.

These memoirs cover the three years Leeflang spent in the United States, including his travels as far west as Kelley, Iowa, where he lived on farms and worked as a farmhand for over two years. At the start he seemed to see the New York City area as his permanent residence. Using an assumed name to avoid being traced by the authorities, he sought shelter in a seaman's refuge in Hoboken, New Jersey, and, after inadvertently being recorded as a native of Holland, Michigan, by a personnel clerk where he sought employment, he blended into the metropolis.

Leeflang quickly obtained a job as a streetcar motorman at $5.00 per day for a seven-day week. He soon moved from the seaman's home to his own private room and his future seemed bright. He had been hired because of high absenteeism of regular motormen suffering from a flu epidemic. In three weeks the regular employees began returning to work so Leeflang lost his job.

Necessity drove him to seek employment through a private agency that recruited workers, mostly laborers, for industry. A laborer's job with Bethlehem Steel Company, obtained through the private placement service, required going into debt for railroad fare to the plant in Johnstown, Pennsylvania. On the train he began an association with Jörgen Dahl, another illegal alien, who served as a companion, though sometimes to Leeflang's regret, until well into 1926.

Leeflang advanced through several stages of employment with Bethlehem Steel in Johnstown, but after three months, with his supervisor claiming economic uncertainty growing out of the pending presidential election necessitating layoffs, Leeflang again lost his job. Now he and Jörgen Dahl talked of California and work in the movie industry. A shortage of money for the trip to Hollywood led them to hitchhiking, which at times seemed to mean more hiking than hitching. Since hoped-for jobs in Cleveland and Toledo failed to materialize, the rosy enticement of Hollywood and the movies gave way to the gray reality of farm work in the trans-Mississippi area.

Hopping freight trains was to replace hitchhiking, but Leeflang and Dahl lacked the skills to mount the moving trains and to evade the railroad detectives. More than once either their dress, demeanor, or easily identifiable foreign origin caused the railroad security agents to be lenient, and they received only warnings to stay off the trains. They returned to the highways for more hitching and hiking.

After a brief interlude in Sturgis, Michigan, to replenish their money supply through Dahl's poker skills, they passed through Chicago and paused in Cedar Rapids, Iowa. There they joined a group of migrant corn pickers who planned to find work in the central part of the state. The experienced members of the group instructed the newcomers in freight train travel and they rode to Boone where the group divided, with Leeflang and Dahl going to Kelley. A Kelley barbershop served as an unofficial employment office; they stated they wanted work and the barber urged his farmers-in-residence to provide jobs. Both Leeflang and Dahl were directed to farmers who needed hands and they settled in for an extended stay in the Kelley area.

The persistent influence of his urban background in Rotterdam and two years of farm work convinced Leeflang that he should not make farming a career. He departed for Chicago where he quickly qualified to drive a cab. For six months he prospered at his job and delighted in Chicago as "the finest town" he had ever lived in. Suddenly prosperity and delight ended. An Immigration Service officer apprehended him and he spent several unpleasant days in the Cook County jail. His former employer in Iowa aranged bail for a brief release until he had to report to Ellis Island for deportation. With that Leeflang's American odyssey came to an end.

WALTER HOUF
Professor of American History
Drake University

American Travels of a Dutch Hobo   1923 - 1926

New York City

> A bum loafs,
> sits and does not wash,
> A tramp loafs,
> walks, and washes his face,
> A hobo moves,
> works, and . . . he is clean.

ASSUME I did belong to the latter and—well, just read!
We live in the year of our Lord 1923.
Hello Manhattan!
Having crossed the big pond we nearly have reached New York port. The ship's telegraph jingles "half speed ahead"; we are steaming up the river Hudson. I signal my TR to the coast station of Long Island and close down my station. When I have finished, I switch off my radio apparatus. I look outside the porthole. We are approaching Manhattan. Abreast of us is Ellis Island, the place where often a lot of immigrants have to await their fate—admission to the U.S.A. or return to the old country. To the left is Staten Island, ahead, Bedloe's Island, carrying the Statue of Liberty, pointing to heaven with its torch. I read about it; this statue, a present of France to free America, is made of 225 tons of copper and iron. The French people raised $450,000 to pay the statue; the Americans raised $350,000 for the pedestal.
The imposing skyscrapers grow bigger and bigger and they force me to keep on looking. They demand all my attention. It is fascinating, this skyline. I have seen lots of towns and cities on my trips, ugly ones and nice ones. But I have never seen anything like this before in my life. It looks like a chain of high mountains, speckled with myriads of glittering eyes. Two tops, towering above the summit, high up in the air, are—they told me later—the buildings of 5th Avenue and those in front later proved to be those of Wall Street. It sets one to thinking to know that human hands created these giants and that the creatures belonging to these hands are swarming beneath, muddling about like ants and probably no longer aware of the fact that they themselves wrought these colos-

3

Seen from the seaside,
Manhattan lies before you as
a high bastion, a parapet of
piers entrenched as if it will
try to stop you from putting
into port between the tow-
ering concrete blocks. When
you look to their tops from
below, it is like they bend
over to each other to cover
you up. You feel small but
protected. Although . . . sup-
pose there comes an earth-
quake! You must not think of
that. Manhattan is built on
rocks.

---

suses. Looking at Manhattan, approaching it from the sea, comes over on you like you're ending a voyage of discovery, finally landing on the shores of some unknown country. One gets a mind to find out what lies behind those concrete blocks.

We arrive at our berth, where our tugboat will stay for another five days. We moor to Pier 21.

Yesterday, our second day in New York, I went with the crew to Coney Island, the big festival park of New York. A ship's crew always seems to seek pleasure in the first place.

From our landing stage we first had to pass the controlling porters and to show our seaman's pass. We strolled along part of the way until we could take a streetcar to 42nd Street and Broadway, from where we took the subway (the BMT) to Brooklyn. Here we called on Kommer, an acquaintance of the first engineer, from whose house we went further with the El to Coney Island, situated on the coast of Brooklyn.

In Coney Island there was a hurly-burly of rides, freaks, food, drinks, and sand. You can have fun with all kinds of moving things in the amusements park. You can play Skee-Ball, quoits, and other games. All admissions cost one nickel. You can descend into a coal mine and ride around in a donkey cart in pitch dark. We had a lot of fun in the steeplechase,

where, on entering, a heavy storm wind tries to throw you off your feet and immediately thereafter you land on a floor that collapses all of a sudden, the fright of which discharges itself in a horrible screaming.

We drank a "bullpup," a mixture of orange juice, peppermint, and gingerale. Then we went into the giant wheel. When we were on top, quite high into the air—at least a hundred feet—we had a magnificent view on Brooklyn. We had not much time to look around, for, on some unexpected moment the compartment in which we were seated made a near somersault and caused us to hold our breath. It sure was lucky we had a safety belt. But when our fright was over we much enjoyed swinging to and fro on this height. There also was a waxen figure gallery. We strolled along the beach, in the creeks of which in warm nights the New Yorkers stay to sleep in the open or at least try to do so. "On hot Sundays," Kommer related, "Coney Island was the most concentrated area of massed humanity."

We had a well-spent evening. Kommer was a good guide; he led us to whatever place we'd like to go. He was an old friend of the first engineer. I cannot hit upon his family name—a boy from Maassluis in southern Holland married here in New York with a pretty American girl, with whom he built here his love nest. They had no children. Emily, his lovely wife, went with

5

us. We finally altogether went into the rolling coaster, the "Big Dip." Emily got seated beside me in the cart and when this raced down with a dizzy speed, she held me tight with her supple arms around my neck, screaming with sensation. I just let her that way during the breathtaking ride. It was my first pleasant encounter with a member of the fair sex in America.

We went to have another drink and very soon conversation started when we were served with a drink unknown to me—root beer—like bullpup, free of alcohol, for America was made dry. Kommer related that in the midtown in the skyscrapers of Broadway and Wall Street the offices of big business were situated. Those of the smaller concerns could mainly be found around 5th Avenue, Park Avenue, and Madison Avenue, somewhere between 42nd Street and 57th Street. Here was the top of New York business life. The top men themselves lived near Central Park and in Long Island, the middle and lower classes in the West Side, Queens, and Brooklyn.

Kommer also told us there were about 250 streets in Manhattan, the houses numbering from south to north. Fifth Avenue divides the East and the West Side. The richest quarter is that of Washington Square, most millionaires and billionaires living there. If you rented a house, you were compelled to take also the furniture that is in it. This is perhaps the reason why you don't see many removing vans in the streets. People crept into their new dwelling with everything in it that's left by the former tenant. It therefore is not very domesticated with somebody else's furniture to live in.

"Everything," he said, "was bought on terms and the women here were the most emancipated creatures in the world, polluting the minds of the teenagers with their depravity of morals. He could not get used to it. There was a thing, however, he'd get ecstasies about, namely, that one out of every fifteen Americans owned an automobile, a car, often a Ford T-model, called in popular terms "Tin Lizzies."

Most drunks and dope fiends in the world are to be found in New York. Walking through the Bowery you could see them stumble about or lying in a corner on the sidewalk. To them it did not matter whether they would be dead or alive. They swallowed their alcoholics until they got the snakes and then mostly it was done with them.

Most married couples had a job, husband and wife and also the kids; the latter to earn some pocket money. Everything here is going to be mechanized. A great deal of the industrial concerns already have come to use the transport belt, while others prepare to do so. Ford was the first to introduce it. This can no more be altered. America is the land of the Tailor system, which is adopted with all its consequences. America is the land of rationalization and, of course, of the almighty dollar! If you wanted to work—in whatever job—you always could, even if it were a job as a dishwasher in one of the many restaurants. You need not show any diploma if you just achieved what you had to do and did your job well, the way you were instructed. Anyhow, Kommer did love New York and he would not in the world like to leave it.

This time I had gone no farther than Coney Island with the crew. I intended to see more of New York later, but I sure had opened my eyes and ears widely.

On the third day of our stay in New York, the old man gave me permission to go ashore alone. I had made an appointment with Kommer that we should go and see a baseball game this afternoon at the Yankee Stadium. "You shouldn't have missed this," he had said. It was early in the morning when I left the ship. The first thing I did was to turn my steps to what in my eyes was the most legendary bridge in the world, the Brooklyn Bridge. I had to see this first of all. As a little boy in my parental home I had seen a reproduction of the effigy of the bridge on a linen tablecloth a friend of my father, an able seaman, had brought with him from America as a present to my folks. I also remembered that Max (that was his Christian name) brought us a box of Turkish Delight, a delicious sweet he must have bought together with the tablecloth in the Syrian quarter along Washington Street. On the fiery red tablecloth the big bridge was printed in all its glory. I never got rid of the impression this picture had made upon me. Now I was here, I'd like to confront my youth's conception with the reality. I took a streetcar running in the direction of Park Row, where the bridge begins on the Manhattan side. It ends on the Brooklyn side near Sands Street. The bridge has two El tracks, two streetcar tracks, a common traffic road, and two sidewalks for pedestrians. Having walked over the bridge one quarter of its length till about the spot where a number of benches invited tired pedestrians to sit down and have a rest, I turned around and gazed at the skyline of Manhattan. My boy's dream had become reality; it was terrific. Farther to the north lies the Manhattan Bridge and still farther the Williamsburg Bridge. It was not given to the designer of the Brooklyn Bridge to live and see the realization of his creation. He died on the bridge under construction on account of an accident. His son, who was chief engineer, also was wounded in this accident and he never recovered. Nevertheless, he was able to lead the building operations from his sickbed during the time that was necessary to complete the bridge, which lasted twelve years yet. In 1883 the bridge was ready and since then a great number of desperate men and women committed suicide by jumping from the high bridge into the water. The other day a woman, who had murdered her husband, killed herself that way.

I took a long look at the bridge in its full length and then I went on walking to the Brooklyn bank, sucking up the scenery to the bottom. In Sands Street I took the El to the quarter in which Kommer's house stood. Together we went with the El to Manhattan and then with the Subway to 155th Street, near

---

Roebling, well-known building engineer, developed and perfected modern techniques for the building of safe suspension bridges. He designed the biggest span ever used in the building of suspension bridges, viz., a 1595½ foot span, which he applied to the Brooklyn Bridge. To walk over the bridge from either side you have to pass a high gate like that of a big castle and far beyond there's another one like it. Since its inauguration the high bridge tempts many a suicider to commit the act of self-destruction by jumping deep down into the water. And the ferries underneath hardly notice it.

8th Avenue. In this part of New York lies the Yankee Stadium. It is the biggest baseball stadium of the U.S.A.

I had never seen a game like baseball. The principles of it kind of compared with the boy's game we used to play in the streets of Rotterdam, where I was born, and which game we called "Sanny plakken." In our game we used, instead of a ball, a piece of a wooden stick about six-inches long and sharpened at both ends. We called this latter the "Sanny." With a "plak," a sort of batting board with a grip as a handle, we tried to hit the Sanny with such force, that the boys who were to catch it couldn't get hold of it. This was for us the opportunity to run our "home run." In the end the loser, standing upright, had to let the plak drop upon one of the sharpened ends of the "sanny"; if he missed, which was often the case, he had to pull out with his teeth a match from a pile of sand in which we had driven it down.

In the Yankee Stadium there was an immense crowd yelling and whistling when Babe Ruth again made one of his famous home runs; it was a grandstand play. Kommer told me about him. He was the most celebrated baseball player of the world, his batting being unequalled. The fabulous Babe did not invent the home run; it became his trademark. The results of his batting were an injection to enhance baseball and it made this branch of sport a very prosperous one in the United States. No wonder that Babe's salary amounted to something like eighty thousand dollars a year, which was more than the salary paid to the president of the U.S.A.

We had a well-spent day. I bought a little baseball trophy as a present to my captain on my way back to the ship. I had sailed a good many years under his command and we made some good trips together over the world. In my secret heart I felt myself a traitor, who bribed someone he needed in his exploits. But I could not resist; the American fever had me in its power.

The fourth day I made a thorough inspection of my board-radio apparatus, so as to ensure it would function all right when the tugboat took the sea again. Everything was in good order, and I reported this to the captain. He then had no objection to my going ashore again. I walked in the direction of Broadway as I wanted to visit the Woolworth Building, 55 storeys, 792 feet high. On the blackboard in the hall I read that you could go up to the highest platform against an admission fee of a quarter; tickets were to be obtained at the lodge of the hall porter. I did so and went up with a special visitors elevator. It was a thrilling spectacle to look deep down at Manhattan and see the small, dark canals in which micro cars were slowly moving and to see a tangle of little points, representing people passing each other. On the other bank of the Hudson—North River—where I saw the quays, I searched for the seaman's home, but I could not detect it from this height.

When I was down again I walked to 5th Avenue, where I took the bus to Central Park. I got out at Columbus Circle near 59th Street; high up in the middle stands the monument of Columbus (1894). Here begins the extensive park. I was surprised about the busy traffic in this region and I wondered if not all New York was riding here around.

Central Park extends from 59th Street to 110th Street, too

far for a walk all the way. I therefore took the bus in the direction of Harlem. All fares on the buses were a dime and I rode more than three miles. In the immense black district of Harlem is a very interesting quarter with lots of peculiar sights; some parts look well-to-do, others very poor.

Walking back to 120th Street, where Columbia University is situated, I again took a bus south. On this ride I saw all kinds of monuments and statues. I alighted at 39th Street and strolled to 7th Avenue, where I saw the Metropolitan Opera. Proceeding to 6th Avenue and from there to 5th Avenue and 33d Street on the corner of which is the famous Waldorf Astoria Hotel, I took the downtown El to the west wall of Battery Park.

There you will find the lively departure point of the ferries to the islands; one goes to the Statue of Liberty, another to Staten Island, to Ellis Island, and other spots. These ferries were big square flatirons that muddled over the water, chased by a streak of black smoke from the funnel midships, typical vessels from which you couldn't tell what was the bow and what was the stern. In the distance you could not see whether they travelled ahead in your direction or sailed away from you. Arriving at their docks they spitted out a great number of people, who hastily spread in all directions. More is the pity I did not have time to make a boat trip. And so I went to look for a hotdog stand, for I was hungry and I ate one of those tasty bites using a little too much mustard, what I washed away with a black coffee. This cost altogether fifteen cents.

I now approached Chinatown, which lies to the west side of the Bowery. Chinatown is situated between Mott-Pell and Doyer Street and west of the Bowery at Chatham Square. I had to cross a bridge from Chatham Square to Mott Street from where I came into the heart of Chinatown. At the end of Pell Street, on the east side, I turned into a sidestreet. In the middle of this rather narrow street, I saw a number of red doors that stood open, the interior dimly lighted. A nauseous sweet scent escaped to the outside from some of the door openings. I once before had sniffed in a smell like this. I couldn't remember where, but I believe it was in Singapore, where I was out on shore leave, our tugboat being in repair. Opium, it dashed through my mind. I peeped into the darkness behind the doors and saw a person stretched out on a bench like a corpse. The goner supported with a white hand a long pipe with a small bowl at the end, from which a streak of yellowish smoke ascended. I thought it lugubrious and I got kind of chilly, when from some dark doorway an old Chinaman shuffled in my direction—a wee bit with the stereotype oriental grin on his face. "Fi' dollah', mistel," he whispered. I was astonished. I had to come to myself for a moment. "Not in fi' centulies, sil," I muttered back. I turned to the right about. No sir, I thought, you won't get me in.

A street further I saw lots of stores and little honky-tonky shops all decorated with Chinese characters, selling fruit and vegetables and all kinds of trash, beside shops of better standing, showing nice objects of jade, Japan-lacquered things, peignoirs, and kimonos. Via Pell Street I went back to the Bowery and walking under the viaducts of the El I came to Division Street near to the Jewish quarter, where I looked at the variety of shops—fur shops and fashion stores—and I witnessed the cheerful and busy bustle. It was crossed by a number of side streets having the appearance of slums, which indeed they were. Once in awhile a train bounced above my head and in the middle of the road there was much car traffic. I decided to make a little trip with the El going south and at some places the train made such sharp curves, like the one at Coenties slip, that people toppled over and had to hold tight to the benches. At Coenties slip I could see part of the port and I saw ships I knew about where they came from. I got off at Fulton Street where the Atlantic fishers deliver their catch at the end of the street where the market is.

From the fish market I walked back again to the Bowery, which quarter I thought quite interesting, and I came back to where I had started. Here the Bowery was crowded with a medley of shops, the owners of which pulling you up in trying to sell you their merchandise. There were bars (free of alcohol!) and small, cheap hotels and boarding houses. Once in awhile I was confronted with a tramp, pale as death, his nose purple. Too much booze? No, too much spirituous; these tramps didn't have the money to buy illegal liquor. I already knew from Kommer that you could only get illegal whisky in the so-called "speak-easies." You'd got to pay a high price for it. A courteous girl, smiling sweetly and wobbling her hips, looked at me invitingly; she carried a red lady's bag. The light girls often make use of the cheap rooms in the little hotels. The rent for a room for the night is fifteen to twenty cents. Of course the hooker sees to it that they pay their rent; the rooms enable them to do their job and provide for their livelihood and that of their bullies, who "own" the girls. I sure was convinced that

Fifth Avenue is an avenue of standing. For all that, fully loaded trucks drawn by horses jolt through the stately thoroughfare and stray aristocrats behind the windows of the Waldorf-Astoria look at them, perhaps with more interest than they do at their Rolls-Royces. A column of watch posts stands in front of the Waldorf-Astoria Hotel in the shape of a row of gold-crowned lanterns, the lights of which add to the glory of wealth housed within this old hotel.

many of these so-called hotels for the greater part were creep joints, as they were called, what meant that amorous males were apt to get robbed there.

I got tired; I should have liked to walk through Greenwich Village, but I thought it better to do this another time. Walking back to Battery Park I came to Bowling Green. Looking in the direction of lower Broadway, I saw the spire of the Singer

Building and diagonally behind it the Woolworth Building with its four elevators, which I had climbed already. I reached Wall Street, the financial centre of the world. Devout amidst the high facades of the big offices, stood Trinity Church as a little oasis of rest.

With the subway I went to 14th Street and back to my ship. I had made my decision. Tomorrow it will happen.

In his lodge the harbor porter looks at me with a bored face. He yawns when I show him my seaman's pass again. With a motion of his hand he waves me out, what means: You may go. That's the guy of the Dutch tugboat who just wants to go ashore to buy something; he'll be back all right.

The big idea! Did he know!

I have withdrawn only ten dollars from my pay to prevent to arouse suspicion and I put on a double set of underwear. Sauntering to the exit of the hall I leave the lodge behind me. If I do not enter this hall again I make myself punishable to the Dutch maritime rules as a deserter and at the same time just as punishable to the laws of the U.S.A. as an illegal immigrant.

But the die is cast. I won't come back. Manhattan has taken hold of me. There's one more thing. In my mind I review, as I had done several times before, what the managing director of the French radio company I was engaged with and who had detached me to the tugboat would say again when I applied to him for my wage: "Sorry boy, we had to lower the wages again because the costs are soaring high." "No lower pay for me this time, mister. It will cost you a whole lot more to engage an American substitute and you will have to pay him in dollars."

It goes to my heart to jump ship. I can't help it; it is the pull of the American dream that has me in its grip. Besides, there could not be a better moment. I am fully aware of the fact that a runaway seaman should never be employed again on whatever ship of Dutch nationality. This is the end of my seaman's career.

I have to walk quite a ways to Christopher Street, where I take the Lackawanna ferry to Hoboken. The first American I came into conversation with I met on the ferryboat, where I asked him the way to the seaman's home in Hoboken. I planned to stay there some time till I got a job. His dress was kind of shabby; he wore a checkered shirt, opened at his neck. His face was frank and he had a kind-hearted smile. We immediately had a spirited talk about the old country he was aching to visit but never came to it. When the ferry arrived in the dock on the Hoboken side he gave me some good advice among which you should remain in the back the first time till you are used to your new surroundings. We parted with a firm handshake.

To me Hoboken was a magic word. Any sailor who ever was on shore leave in New York had once been to the Seaman's Mission. The Seaman's Home is controlled by the Dutch Reformed church, who manages the mission among seamen, giving them all the aid they need, as far as possible. If a sailor signs off and wants a job the mission will assist him to the utmost of its ability. This, what they call the Helping Hand Mission, supplies addresses and provides for shelter. This mission naturally tries to persuade you to become a member of the Reformed church. A hobo should always try to get lodging at the mission rather than lie on the floor in some flophouse, for these floors never got cleaned.

I applied at the Seaman's Home to ask for shelter for a couple of nights; they did not turn me down. I met an Englishman, Donald Barton, who also had jumped his ship and who already had a job as a dishwasher in a cafeteria. In the reading room I looked into the ads of the evening papers to see what kind of jobs were offered that might suit me. I ran through a full page of all kinds of common jobs like carpenters, solicitors, junior clerks, etc. I was not in a position to apply for a job with high requirements. I was not familiar with the jobs mentioned in this page, so I went on searching other pages. At last I detected an advertisement in which temporary motor-men were asked for the New York Street Railway (NYSR) to make up for the shortage of manpower on account of a flu epidemic and possibly for a longer period. A short training was necessary during which, however, no pay could be given. This streetcar company seemingly in this way created a sort of reserve to fall back on in case of another shortage. This job attracted me the more so as I knew quite a lot of electricity and motors. I decided to try and tackle this job. Driving an electric streetcar did not seem very difficult to start with in my new career.

I had a good night's sleep at the home and early next morning I went out to get the job. I had to go Manhattan. The

Those ferries—the New Yorkers can't do without. They transport millions and millions of people, hurrying to some goal unknown to others. They spread in all directions, spitted out by those flatboats muddling along the water surface and often wrapped in the smoke their funnels scornfully send after them, like if they would say, Try to do without us!

distance from the Seaman's Home to the Lackawanna ferry was hardly five minutes walk. On the deck of the ferry a shoeshine boy inspected my shoes and concluded these were too dirty to walk with. "Wants a shine, Sir?" he yelled to me. I mounted his high stool and planted my feet on the board. I could look through the square windows behind me. In front I had a wide view on the Hudson.

The ferry jingled and departed for the other side of the river, the west side of Manhattan. When I caught sight of the opposite ferry coming my way, I all of a sudden noticed a few members of the crew, apparently looking in my direction. The shoe-shine boy got dumb with amazement when his queer customer jumped from his high seat to the deck with a tiger's leap. The boy flapped his rag and asked, "Whotsa matta, sir?" "Sh, sh," I warned him, crouching as low to the deck as I could and hiding my head under the benches like if I was looking for something I had lost. "You dropped something, sir?" the boy asked again. Some passengers who stood beside me also began to search the deck for some lost object. When I peeped stealthily at the ferry that now was disappearing, he grasped the situation. These boys are no fools; they know their customers. He could not finish my shoes as the time was up. "What do I owe you?" I asked him. "A dime sir, shouldn't I get it done?" "No," I said, "Leave it that way." I pressed a dime in his hand and said, "you may finish it when you see me again."

Once more I looked at the river. My attention was arrested a few moments by what was happening on the river. A tugboat of Moran pushed against the sides of a big two-funneled ship. Those little push-pull tugboats are the draft horses of this world port. No matter how big the ship, they tackle the job to get them docked or out of their berth. I would not have to board a tugboat anymore. I was a land rat by this time and I need no longer listen out to ships in distress and I no longer was asked to help a hand in hauling the hawser.

I had crossed the Rubicon. I hurried ashore and disappeared in the crowd, which is not so difficult in New York and certainly not on the busy waterfront of the West Side.

First thing I did was to drop in at Thompson's cafeteria in Christopher Street, a self-service restaurant. I ate a number of doughnuts and poured a cup of coffee, what cost me fifteen cents totally. It was the first time I had entered a cafeteria where you could serve yourself to whatever food or drink you liked. It confirmed my opinion about the business mindedness of the Americans.

When I left the eating house I took my bearings in the direction of 14th Street. This street appeared to be not far from the ferry docks. Again I looked at the other side of the river. They're sure on their way to the Seaman's Home in search for me, I thought, thinking of the crew. I had changed my name to prevent that they should find out my hiding place. The letter I left in my cabin, addressed to my captain, stated: "Don't look for me, you won't find me." I had to prove this and to keep out of sight. I did regret I had to take leave of the old man this way, for he was a darned nice fellow.

Fourteenth Street was easily found. It is rather easy to find the way in New York. You just have to count from the first to the umptieth street. They form blocks from street to street, diagonally crossed by the avenues. Twenty street blocks measure one mile; so do seven avenue blocks. Fourteenth Street crosses many avenues. Where 14th Street crosses 3rd Avenue you can see Irving Place to the right. This part of 14th Street formerly used to be famous for its attractions. Early this century there even was an opera building that burned down later and there was an academy of music. Now there were a number of theaters. Quite near to where I was walking was a vaudeville theater. In this part of 14th Street there was a lively bustle and some pleasant excitement, especially around the theaters. Everywhere the street crossings showed a busy traffic. The busiest crossing I had ever seen, however, was that of 42nd Street and 5th Avenue. I had seen this crossing already when I was out with the crew. I remember that in the middle of this crossing a traffic cop regulated traffic coming from all directions. Most traffic cops looked sturdy and well-to-do and many of them had a fat appearance. I never had seen cops like them in Rotterdam or London.

The busy traffic in the main streets of New York drove noisily past me. The cars bumped over the manholes in the streets, from which live steam poured out. I could not quite gather what it was that made the steam. I thought it came from the subway. In the short time I walked I already had heard a number of police-car sirens and fire bells mingling with the traffic noise.

It was about ten o'clock when I applied at the office of the streetcar company on 14th Street near Broadway. It was an unimpressive office building. I joined a row of applicants that stood there already. After awhile the row had grown behind me to a respectable length. A guy behind me tried to push me aside trying to get before me, but one day in the roaring life of New York allowed me to make clear that I should not tolerate this and my English seemed to be sufficient to underline this. Most of them were aliens who were not able to speak a decent word of English.

In less than one hour the long row before me was worked off and came my turn. A clerk called me to his desk. "Name? Birthdate?" "Where you come from?" "*Holland.*" "Holland, Michigan?" I did not quite understand what he meant, what lead the clerk to write this down. So, I was classified that I came from Holland in the state of Michigan and not from the Netherlands. Well, I left it that way.

"First door to the right". He pointed to a door that stood open. "Hurry-up, next is waiting." I had to move quickly. It was a dingy little room I entered. In the middle stood a man in a white coat. "Lower your pants," he ordered. He proved to be a doctor. Everything was executed in a record of time. He sank his fingers in my lower belly and looked at my genitals. "All right, get a move on please, hurry up." (This hurry up doings seem to be their pet sayings.) Pulling up my pants I took a rush to another room; it was just like a little game that was played—hide-and-seek from one room to another. The last room I was ushered in they pushed a cap—a kind of a kepi— upon my head. It was far too small. Then I got one that sank over my ears, then again one that pinched my forehead, and at last one that fitted me. Another clerk shoved a sheet of paper under my very nose. "Would you sign this, please?" I scribbled my name. They then handed me a booklet with instructions, the contents of which I had to impress upon my memory. And finally they gave me a paper, stating that I had to report at the depot of 14th Street Division next day at six o'clock in the morning to start getting instruction to become a motorman. The first three days I did not get any money. When I should qualify on the fourth day my pay would be five dollars a day with ten working hours, seven days of the week. If I did not qualify, I got the boot. I was allowed free admittance to all cars of the division, provided I wore my cap with the badge. Motorman in New York! It sure was something entirely different from what I was used to. Then, sailing on a ship, now, driving a streetcar; then, the Morse key, now, the coffee grinder—so they called the switch cupboard containing the live wires for the electric current that sets the streetcar to move. To actuate the current a handle was used that slid over a number of copper contacts.

In the Seaman's Home nobody had inquired after me, which was a load off my mind.

Next day, things had a queer start. The father of the home had omitted to have me awakened at five o'clock in the morning. I hardly slept that night, lying awake most of the time for fear to come too late, but on some evil moment I had dozed off. I awoke with a shock exactly at a quarter past five; lucky enough just in time to dress and catch the ferry. "Darn it, hurry up." (I already had adopted the phrase.) Coffee, doughnuts in the cafeteria, rushing to the ferry I need not hide now: no crew was ever to set out that early, unless they were tipsy and still on their way to their ship. Well, then I'd be the first to take my bearings and keep aloof.

I boarded a streetcar—I believe it was in Washington Street—I thought was going in the direction of 14th Street. My uniform cap was to guarantee me a free ride. But not this time! "You've got to pay your nickel or you'll get off!" the conductor snorted. In anger I put my nickel into the slot. And then the streetcar turned around the corner to proceed in quite another direction. It dawned on me that this conductor wore a cap that differed from mine. My cap was flatter. It apparently was a car of a rival company, I thought. One that probably catered for another division. Perhaps the cars of the NYSR only served 14th Street and its surroundings. Or perhaps it was a cooperating company and my free ride was only valid in my own division.

Pondering about all this in a jiffy, I jumped off the streetcar when it stopped at the following block and ran as fast as I could in the direction I thought was the right one. I had guessed well and I reached the depot about five minutes too late. I heard a man raging and scolding and I caught sounds that resembled something like "bastard." "That idiot'd make a fool of me." Then someone in a far corner of the depot shouted, "Sweeney, there's the guy." "Hurry-up you bastard," Sweeney yelled. "I am five minutes late. I got to drive to the bone to cover the lost time; get a move on, you dummy."

And so I stood on the streetcar balcony beside an angry Sweeney, panting and looking. The whole morning of this first day Sweeney went on scolding and he did not quit this, ere I myself had to take the stand behind the coffee grinder and turn the crank. He then began to dictate to me: "one, two, three, . . . off; one, two, three, . . . off; one, two, three, . . . off, brake! One, two, three, . . . off . . . Off, I said. One . . . brake, not so fast, sucker! I was continuously moving the handle—the crank—over the smooth copper contacts and . . . suddenly I had to jam on the brakes . . . "Brake!"—a near hit. I reacted almost immediately and this time Sweeney said nothing and nodded approvingly. The shock caused a guy who stood in the doorway annoyingly staring at a lovely female to bump upon my back. The girl took the opportunity to go and be seated far in the rear. From this distance he would not very well neck her. Within two days I already had the perfect command over the

20

big streetcar. With the Westinghouse brake, a braking system using compressed air, I could quickly bring the car to a standstill and was able to throw over the electric switches— with current to the left, without current to the right.

The technical side of driving a streetcar was not the worst. It was the way people stood behind me, annoyingly looking upon my hands and yelling into my ears all of a sudden and with a voice of thunder—"Ahwannagidovnekstblok." Did I know what they meant with this double Dutch? Did I have to gather they wanted me to stop next block to enable them to get off? People entered the car at the rear end, threw their nickel into the slit of the glass box fixed near the seat of the conductor, who sat on a high stool watching. All he had to do was to open and close the doors and follow the passengers depositing their nickels into his box. He did not change money; there was not time for it, everything was going in a hurry. Everybody entering had to have his nickel ready to hand. If they had not the exact amount, they had to get off or pay more than a nickel with whatever small change they had. The heaviest work he had to do was counting his receipts of the day, put this in little linen bags, and deliver these at the office. You need not have studied economics for this job. The passengers who had entered in the rear had to leave the car in front and had to ask the motorman to stop. As my linguistic capacities were mainly based on my school and seaman's English, the bellowing in my ears had little effect on my actions. So, I imperturbably moved on with my vehicle till the moment Sweeney gave me to understand that he need not fling me off the balcony himself, but that the passengers might do this if I continued to drive on past the stops they'd asked for so they had to walk back, only because I pretended not to hear them. I took good notice of his sarcasm and drove more carefully and listened more attentively when I drove near a stopping place. In Manhattan it seemed to be the custom to have the streetcars stopped at the last house of a block in either direction.

In less than a week I drove my streetcar like if I'd done this all my life. I was a finished motorman. I drove across downtown Manhattan through 14th Street from east to west and vice versa, standing on the balcony and turning my crank and thumping my car over the steel rails. A motorman, earning his first hard-earned pay—five dollars a day, thirty-five dollars a week (at a stretch with no day off). To me it was wonderful and I felt it like something sensational. Once a pitching ship's deck under my feet, now a jolting streetcar balcony. With the contact handle I set the colossus in motion and with another handle manipulating the Westinghouse air-brake I brought it to standstill. In case of emergency I could sprinkle sand on the rails in front of the wheels. In this way I could stop the car almost at once. All day long I drove in 14th Street, from 9th Avenue (west) to East River near the Williamsburg Bridge, vice versa. It was quite a good connection between Hoboken, Manhattan, and Brooklyn.

The Williamsburg Bridge runs from De Lancey Street in the East Side to Broadway in Brooklyn, the borough with the most dense population. This bridge is the biggest suspension bridge in the world. With my streetcar I drove near to the bridge. To drive back, switching was done along East River Park, near De Lancey Street. Looking back into De Lancey Street you could see the viaduct of the El that rode in Allen Street. On the corner of the crossing was the Bank of the U.S.A., a Jewish bank supplying loans to immigrants from the old country who had freshly arrived in Manhattan. It sure had chosen the right place in the heart of the overcrowded Jewish quarter. The surroundings of De Lancey Street and Canal Street were called "Brass Town" because of the many shops selling copper ware.

Soon after I got the motorman's job I moved from the Seaman's Home to a small room, sparsely furnished, in Christopher Street not so far from West 14th Street and Greenwich Village. In earlier days this neighborhood must have been a notorious one, a hook alley, crime running riot here. Now it was a decent little quarter with a few residential streets and a number of streets with queer little shops. Greenwich Village as a whole lies on one side between Washington Square and 14th Street and between 5th and 8th avenues on the other side. It is one of the oldest parts of Manhattan. Someone told me the other day that not so long ago, perhaps ten years, the "night judge" held session of court in the dark hours and passed immediate sentence on every offender who was brought up.

I crossed Broadway several times a day. It sure was the busiest street I had ever seen. And every time again it gave me a thrill to make the crossing with my thundering car, jingling loudly. As a matter of fact, 14th Street crosses all avenues of Manhattan. On the corner of 6th Avenue was the big department store of Macy's. Continually I also passed Union Square, a nice and busy square. The quarters I drove through were alternatively busy, monotonous, and lively. I had ample opportunity to observe the situations around me. The West Side between 9th and 10th avenues was in the vicinity of the North River, not far from the big shipping lines, and was the busiest part. In the middle of 14th Street was the most lively part and in the east—in the neighborhood of the Manhattan Bank opposite Brooklyn—there was more street noise with many hustlers monkeying around.

I drove past a diversity of high buildings, relieved by living quarters with the well-known ugly iron stairs on the outside, blocks of houses straight and dull. You could not walk these streets without getting weary. I got bored with them. It was followed up by a section full of liveliness, especially in the night, with much gay light. In this part of 14th Street there were lots of flashlight advertisements. In East 14th Street there were many restaurants and a number of theaters. I also saw a music hall. I did not only see it, I also heard it. I can't count the times I listened to the most popular hit of the day, "Yes, We Have No Bananas." The former vaudeville theater now was Loew's Picture House. One evening, when I was free, I went to the picture house to see "The Kid," a movie picture with Charlie Chaplin. I also remember they showed "Dreyfus on Devil's Island" and, as an extra, a Russian film.

Adjoining to this moving-picture house, on the right of it, is the Edison Building, where formerly was Tammany Hall—the political center of the New York Democratic party. Originally this center was founded to give the minorities of the different nationalities and races a voice in the political choice of a mayor and of the other authorities who reigned the city. In fact, it had derived from the Tammany Society, a benevolent group that was formed with a view to take care of revolutionary patriots and their kin; this was prior to the Civil War. And it finally exercised important influence on political matters. It opposed the antiimmigrant policies of the Know-Nothings or the Native American Party. The society succeeded in abolishing property ownership as a qualification to vote and in the adoption of the five-year limitation for the acquisition of citizenship. Tammany Hall aided the naturalization of foreigners and it was on this account considered a radical organization. The organization, indeed, had not a social intention but was more inclined to promote the opening up of fallow territory in the country and the settlement of immigrant families. In New York, Tammany Hall had a lot of influence on the Democratic party's municipal policy and in the time of the election of a new mayor there always was much goings on here in 14th Street, for the Tammany Society kind of controlled the New York political patronage.

From 14th Street to De Lancey Street, the streets do no longer follow the straight course; the blocks are no longer square. The streets cross each other and run in all directions. It is kind of hard to find your way here. Fourth Street, for instance, runs in the West Side diagonally through 11th and 12th streets. I had driven my streetcar without any complications for three weeks and I already felt myself adapted to my surroundings and as an integrated part of Manhattan, and I felt quite at ease among the New Yorkers. And then, like a thunderbolt from the blue, the cold shower came. I got fired and many others with me. The sickness rate on account of the flu epidemic had decreased to the extent that all temporary hands, particularly the younger to which I belonged, could hop it. This seemed to be the usual practice; no more pay, only the days I had worked this week. He who had to care for a family and some of the older men were allowed to stay longer for some time to come.

Broadway does not honor its name; it is not as broad as you may think it is. It is wider near Union Square, a pleasant place to linger. Streetcars dominate the driveway and there are many crossings on Broadway. The streetcars do not ride fast and so you have ample time to think about and pick the stores you may go shopping afterwards. A streetcar hurries over the crossing at 14th Street.

I had saved enough money to pay the rent of my room and to keep it on for some more days and to enable me to buy the necessary things. What was left was enough to get through some time.

I had to look for another job and again I looked through the ads in the evening papers, bearing in mind that I had to reckon with my vulnerable position. I therefore could not apply for the more important jobs for the time being. I hoped to be able to prove myself later, so I might convince the authorities to find reasons for legalizing my further stay in the U.S.A. and grant me the first papers, but perhaps all this might be a castle in the air.

Anyway, I had to find a job now. From other inmates of the Seaman's Home I had heard that somewhere in the Bowery and in the lower East Side there were small private labor agencies, which recruited laborers and other working people for the industry, big ones as well as small ones. These petty dealers catered for quite a lot of men for the labor force necessary and when a man was aground, like me, he could make his choice out of a great variety of jobs. The best agencies were to be found about 4th Street in the Lower East Side.

Next day I went that way early in the morning. From Christopher Street I walked to 8th Avenue and took a streetcar to the East Side near De Lancey Street from where I turned my steps in the direction of East Village, passing the Bowery. Going somewhat east I got to Hester Street, the Jewish quarter, like in Amsterdam, but larger and busier. Many Jews wore a Garibaldi hat—a derby—or what they called a kelly. The street was crowded with carts carrying merchandise and along the sidewalks there were innumerable little shops. These Jews traded in a mishmash of goods from fur coats to watermelons. Anything you needed was for sale here. The quarter I walked through seemed to be inhabited with Polish and Russian Jews, but I also saw many Italians. On my way from Hester Street to Essex Street I passed Mulberry Street, a market on wheels. Fruit, fish, and clothing were sold to the teeming population, sitting on the doorsteps and in the windows. The odors and the flies that accompanied the carts were a mere nuisance to anyone who came near. It was a poor street of this quarter. It looked to me that among those who lived in these slums, only the fittest could survive.

I walked till I reached 4th Street. I was near 6th Avenue and as I had not eaten much this morning I decided to have a quick lunch at Pig and Whistles, which cost me fifty cents.

In all big cities there are popular neighborhoods with separate racial or national character, like Hester Street,
where the male population wears kel-
lys, and Mulberry Street, a very poor
quarter of the Lower East Side. Inde-
scribable poverty and eternal hustling
for a livelihood! They form a touching
portrait of tough little folks—a portrait
well-to-do people not for all in the
world would like to get involved with.

Then I walked again into 4th Street. It was a hit immediately. I
observed quite a number of labor agencies, "man catchers"
they called them, and I could make a choice from the jobs
mentioned on the blackboards outside, next to the door.

When I peeped inside and had a good look at the owners,

I'd bet my life that most of them would not be averse to shanghai their "merchandise." But, what of it! If you are badly in need of a job, you could not be particular. One got to have dough to keep alive and my stock of dollars would soon be faded away. And then, what about me? In the gutter in the Bowery? This thought looked unattractive to me.

There were big agencies, apparently the well-to-do-ones, and small ones. I set sail to the agency that had the largest blackboard in front of its window. The jobs were written on it with chalk. Behind the description of the job the pay was mentioned: solicitors, sixty cents (that is the hourly pay); carpenters, eighty cents; skilled laborers, fifty cents to sixty cents; mechanics, seventy cents; unskilled laborers, thirty-eight cents. As I was not familiar with any of these jobs, except perhaps that of laborer, I decided to choose the latter. It would suit me anyway. Come on, let's get in, I said to myself.

These labor joints, not to be mistaken with the official labor exchanges, were as far as I could notice, run for the greater part by Jews from Eastern Europe—Armenians, Poles, and Slovakians. The stuffy little office I entered apparently belonged to an East Jew, I gathered from his name. Chewing on a black cigar stump in the corner of his mouth, the owner growled to me, "Whot d'ye want?" In this situation, new to me, I felt rather uneasy. He seemed to think that a greenhorn like me—which undeniably could be deduced from my appearance—should only be too happy with him as a benefactor, to help out. "Well," I said nervously and possibly a little bluntly to make a firm stand against his indifference, "What else would I be here for than to get a job? But, after all, if you don't like me, I just as well go and look for another affair."

My English, still school seaman's, seemed to impress him. He pulled the cigar stump from his lips and deposited it on a corner of the dingy table. With a stately gesture he spread a sheet of grubby white paper in front of me upon which a variety of jobs were written down. "Nah," he said, "which do you want?" He became more enthusiastic. "Nah," I retorted, "a gentleman's job, laborer!" His zest ebbed away visibly. "Laborer?" He obviously earned the least on those inferior jobs; they seemed to yield not much profit to him. And he probably had estimated me to be of a higher standard. He jerked away the paper, folded it, and said: "How about laborer at the Bethlehem Steel, the Cambria Plant in Johnstown, Pennsylvania, outside labor around the mills, ten hours a day, thirty-eight cents an hour." He explained that if I had no money, the train fare could be advanced, thirteen dollars, which amount had to be paid back against interest of course. He could fix the payments, the installments with the employer, who would cut it down on my pay, a weekly pay. Besides, seven dollars would be deducted for board and lodging. I had to stay in the camp. "You have to remain in the laborer's camp after the working hours, for the time being. If you might happen to do better and got higher pay, you may leave the camp and live on your own if you want to. That's to say, if you're paid off. You must see for yourself. And . . . eh . . . no strike. That is punishable—they mean business. Is this clear? Yes? Well, then sign your name on this here paper," he said. And he went on, "Have you got any money? How much?" "Ten bucks," I said. I had more, but that was none of his business. Well, that's that. You may pitch your tents next door and have something to eat if you like to. Cost you two dollars for both. An expensive bite, I thought. This fellow tried to earn in some way or other extra little money on poor devils like me. "Till tonight," he said, "eight forty-five at the Pennsylvania Station. From there you depart with the whole gang to Johnstown. Have you signed? Here's a copy. That's settled then."

He picked up his cigar stump that still lied stinking on the table and with a wry face put it back between his full lips. And so I was shackled to a dog's job, what I found out later.

I had myself freshened up in the poorly furnished room the man had appraised to me and where I found a number of other victims. They, like me, had in this odd way made acquaintance with the rare scale of opportunities to get admittance to the American labor market. I tried to calculate what the shark of this labor agency might earn on people who were on the rocks. He must have had at least ten clients a day, for, behind me some other guys had come in and been waiting for me to hook it. I assumed he sure would earn ten dollars per client, preconceiving he would "catch" ten fellows that would make one hundred dollars a day. To earn this amount of money I had been standing on the balcony of a jolting streetcar for three weeks at a stretch, with the fear in my legs for the prospect of a near collision. Maybe I might have done the same this fellow did if I'd have had a chance.

Before my time, an immense stream of immigrants must

have entered the United States in the nineties. From this flock the present law-abiding citizens originated. They had to work hard for their and their family's existence. Often the elderly people were exploited by unscrupulous employers, who, in their turn dictated conscienceless crimps. Maybe this gave rise to the establishment of these private labor agencies. It looked to me there always must have been an army of unemployed and of idlers in the New World, most of them the misfits, the tramps, the lazy bums, the alcoholics, and the dope fiends. Those of the bunch who succeeded in being set on their feet again, maybe once in a while applied for work at these labor agencies.

Strolling in 4th Street I was confronted with the man who I already met in the Seaman's Home, Donald Barton. He stopped and said: "I'm looking for another job 'cause I've got to get out of New York. There were some men of the immigration, I believe. They came to the Mission, I think, it was a kind of a silent razzia. I believe we're hot. You too, should keep out of the mission." "Thanks," I said, "I won't be there anymore. I've a job in Pennsylvania. You'll get a job all right. Well, be good to yourself, goodbye."

I proceeded my walk. At East 4th Street there were a lot of little shops, bars, and dancings. I tried to get a beer in one of the bars; in vain though. The rest of the day I availed myself of the opportunity to go sightseeing in New York and feast upon unexpected impressions of this metropolis. To be sure, New York is no more America than Paris is France and London is England. But you got to have been there to be able to compare it with other parts of the country to learn what America really is.

Greater New York consists of five districts, the boroughs: Manhattan, Brooklyn, the Bronx, Queens, and Staten Island. They each have their own characteristics. New York's charm lies in its restlessness, it's dynamics. As a newcomer your first impression is one of loneliness, like if you are excluded from society; you have to find your own way amidst all those hasty people who hurry to a certain goal. People seemed to multiply here in fast pace. I never saw a city so overcrowded.

Looking at the opposite bank of East River, I saw Queens, seemingly under the stress of a building boom. In Queens alone live nearly a million people. I became infatuated with the crowds that pounced upon the subway, the El, the streetcars, and the buses. But then if you accost a person, either a man or a woman, to ask the way, they are very human and friendly even if they are in a hurry. And all of a sudden you no longer will feel lonesome. You wonder how all this is to be reconciled with the inhuman rhythm of this giant city. It is all liveliness, changing; even the concrete buildings have a face that changes on set times. You feel like you are liberated when you knock about this city amidst the American crowd. You collaborate, you're going to make it!

The Lower East Side lodges a conglomerate of races. Seventy years ago when there was not any law on immigration, tens of thousands of immigrants arrived here from Europe. They came to Manhattan by sailing vessel. Packed like herrings in the wrecky ships, thousands of them deceased mainly because of illness during the crossing. The trips across the Atlantic sometimes could last several weeks and even months. A whole lot of these miserable migrants became the first bums, many of whom drifted into the slums or died in the work-houses or in other Poor Law institutions.

American life, as I see it, is organized in a refined manner. But something of mental poverty can be felt when you look at the clamorous advertisements, the technical utilities, and the uniformity of the clothing and of the eating habits. At the many frankfurter stands everywhere you can eat your hotdog and the cooked corn ears. Altogether, it does not appear as snug as things are in Europe. Flashlight ads and noisy newspaper headlines are directed at mass sales and money making more than at the cultural aspects of life. A uniform standarized kind of living pattern without much purpose. Still, the average American lives dynamically, even though his thinking is directed at facts and money, at films and popcorn, at cars and root beer. If he relaxes, he not only is well mannered but also very human and always ready to help those who are in need. America, and particularly a town like New York, is a melting pot for immigrants, with hard spelling rules. All the same, the immigrants were, and still are, those who made America to what it is—a mighty conglomerate of races with altogether one general characteristic, the American.

You can distinguish different gradations in the classes of population: the upper ten, the upper four hundred, who strike the keynote; the middle class (with upper and lower strata); and the lower class (also with upper and lower strata). The Negroes, Puerto Ricans, Mexicans, and the immigrants from the Middle East represent a class apart, not accessible for the white race. Hence the ghettos. Anyhow, whatever class one may belong to, in social intercourse they are still the same. People are on friendly terms with each other, notwithstanding the difference in rank in society, and they call each other with their Christian name almost as soon as they meet each other. Everyone goes to the cafeterias, buys the same suits, drives the same cars—if they have one, and then mostly on terms.

This uniformity of living habits in the U.S.A. causes the immigrant to feel at ease very soon. The European design soon gets overhauled, touched up, and attuned to the new customs, generally bent on making money. Conceitedness is defied and cultural background comes in the second place; therefore the intellectual elite stands somewhat beside the majority of the people. But there is always the menace among the lower class of getting idle and getting classified among the derelicts of the Bowery. And so it is already since the first immigrants landed in Manhattan.

Those who were able to maintain themselves, became for the most part respectable citizens. Today, the calendar says 1923, you'll still find in the Bowery the derelicts, the dope

---

Madison Square Gardens would not have been built if there had not been rodeos, circuses, and boxing matches. The interests of the public are many sided. Those who are western inclined go to the rodeo. These rodeos meant torment to the horses and still bigger torment to the cowboys, but the latter are paid for it! Those who like to look breathlessly to the trapeze workers go to circuses. Those who spend their evening to see boxers with cauliflower ears beat their opponents swollen eyebrows and black eyes, eagerly pay their admission fee to get their sadistic satisfaction when the opponent of their favorite goes down.

fiends, and the alcoholics who try to wrest a nickel from you to buy booze or drugs. The Bowery shelters many aliens; people who came from the four winds to try their luck and illegal immigrants, like me, who stay and work here secretly.

Many of them have no work or don't want any work and pass their time with loafing and fuddling themselves. It is a puzzle to me how they got the money to buy the stuff. Crime is evident in these surroundings and has increased since America was made dry. Pussyfoot has a lot to answer for since he, unaware of its negative influence on man, pleaded for prohibition, which finally led to the complete prohibition of alcoholic drinks all over the country. This in its turn promoted and facilitated the revival of crime and aroused the slumbering gangsterdom. The Mafia took advantage of the possibilities to slip through the meshes of the law and they had their gorillas and their racketeers with their guns under the armpit to intimidate recalcitrant clients who did not want to pay in time. They did not earn money on the alcoholics of the Bowery. These were less than the underdogs; the slums were not their territory. They found most profits in the restaurants and in the speakeasies in the better situated districts. Sometimes the

police interfered. Crime was firmly organized, however, and the gangs were active in every part of New York.

I had all afternoon to see New York at leisure before I turned my back on this gigantic agglomeration. New York comprises nearly two hundred towns and communities within a radius of sixty miles. The living quarters outside the city boundaries are formed by the suburbs, in which most of the better situated people are living. They are for their existence committed to work in the city and add to the crowds that invade Manhattan. They hurry to the subway to go to this mad, uproarious, excited, brilliant city. They form an avalanche, moving continually into anonimity. One out of every twenty Americans live in or around New York, the population of which having been generated or originated from no less than sixty nationalities and races. Between themselves the Yankees do discriminate as to the races, although you won't perceive this in daily life. How some of the descendants of different races are called by the men in the street I found out already: a Chinese, a chink (a slit eye); a Mexican, a greaser; an Italian, a wop or a dago; a Czech, a bohunk; a Negro, a nigger; a man from the country, a gill; an Englishman, a limey; a Pole, a polack; the man from Texas calls the New Yorkers snow diggers, and so on.

New York is a megalopolis with a mountain range along the waterfront. Behind it a million population, one quarter of which live in dark, dirty houses with storeys piled up high and on the outside, rusty iron fire escapes. Most of them are in Brooklyn and in the Lower East Side of Manhattan. The Bowery, Brooklyn, Hoboken, Queens, Coney Island, and the big bridges I had seen already. With the subway I went to 42nd Street and Broadway; when I came out of the underground tunnel, I looked over Broadway and saw the famous Ziegfeld Follies, the leg show they called it; big posters showed the folly girls with their nicely shaped legs.

What I further did like to see as yet was the part of Manhattan between 42nd Street and 60th Street, where Central Park is and where you find all those little restaurants that will serve you a good meal, not too expensive. In a little Bohemian affair I ate a well-done steak and swallowed a milkshake, a novelty I tasted for the first time in my life. Then I went to Greenwich Village, a precious part of New York, with lots of bazaars and little stores and drugstores where you can buy all kind of delicious ice-cream sodas and where you see a multitude of sauntering people, like in Paris on the boulevards.

I am living in a dream. All things went so fast. I have not lived—I am living. Living by the American dream, which exercises on me like on many others a magnetic force, the attraction of which I could not resist and by which all thoughts of the past become blurred. In Greenwich Village I came back to reality, to Europe. I wanted to undergo the atmosphere, to taste the radiation around it and therefore took a streetcar that drove me from 5th Avenue to Washington Square. Around this square one of the oldest parts of Manhattan is concentrated, junky, and colorful. A lot of streets run crisscross through each other, contrary to the streets in other quarters, which run orderly in straight, square blocks. It is the place where musicians, painters, and other real and fake artists reside and get together—the Bohemians—who run bizarre little shops. Here you will see protruding house fronts and little balconies. I got into the Woolworth 5-and-10-cents store, where one could buy a whole lot of trifling things very cheaply.

The surroundings of 6th Avenue and 4th Street formerly were notorious for the crimes that were committed there. Since the Bohemians, artists, and modernists invaded here, all things have changed and crime left to take hold of the Bowery and Harlem. Once again I walked from Greenwich Village to Mott Street to have another look at Chinatown. In one of the streets I observed the American-Chinese church, the "True Light" Lutheran church with on the front wall the inscription in Chinese characters beside the American version.

Having seen Chinatown, which consists of about three street blocks, I took the subway to the busiest point of New York, the street crossing of 42nd Street and 5th Avenue, where I, coming to street level, saw Saint Patricks Cathedral (with 2500 seats). Then I went to look into the big hall of the Grand Central Station, a magnificent terminal. This, however, was not the station I had to go to. The trains to Pennsylvania depart from the Pennsylvania Station in 7th Avenue.

Walking further quite a distance to the junction of Broadway and 5th Avenue, I looked up at the Flat Iron Building on the corner of 23rd Street. They had told me that at stormy weather it shakes quite a bit. It is said its top may move two feet to and fro and it had happened in the past that the windowpanes broke and went down so that people beneath got hurt. When I crossed the square I nearly collided with Jan

Andriessen, a former shipmate of mine on one of the Van Uden ships. With me he sailed as a cook on board of the steamship "Lekhaven." He, too, had signed off. I had not met him for quite many years. It looks like even in the busiest parts of world cities, where you would not expect it at all, seamen meet each other. He now worked as a cook in one of the big restaurants, the name of which slipped from my mind. I thought it wise not to renew the bonds to prevent possible detection. We parted with a firm handshake.

My time is up. I have to go back. I cannot afford to miss my train. I must be at the station at half-past eight. The whole gang was present in the hall. We board the train to Johnstown, Pennsylvania.

Good-bye New York!

Johnstown, Pennsylvania

THREE COMPARTMENTS were reserved for our transport to Pennsylvania. The train route would run from Manhattan via the railroad tunnel under the Hudson, past Jersey City, Newark, through the Blue Ridge mountains to Scranton, and from there via a level track to Johnstown. Here we would again come into a kind of mountainous area. There were no sleeping places, for they had chosen for the cheapest way of travelling.

Fate was with me. I secured a corner seat, which I did not give up anymore. With my jacket rolled up under my head I could quietly await the night. Opposite of me the corner seat was taken by a Norwegian who introduced himself as Jörgen Dahl. Next to me a man was seated who was not so young; I guessed he must have been about forty. His face was wrinkled and he undeniably was a Yankee, his extending chin having the distinctive features of the American who has spoken his Anglo-Saxon from the time he was born. He spoke kind of boisterously, laying the emphasis on "you bet your life," and he told me of his having been a truck driver by profession, being a member of the driver's union.

"What job are you going into?" he inquired. "I go as a laborer around the plant," I said. "A lousy job; you'd better be a driver like me. You bet your life. You've always work. I'm gonna drive lorries in the steel mill, sixty cents an hour, good pay, you bet your life." "I believe so," I said, "it's a better job than mine. I can't drive trucks or lorries, but I can drive streetcars."

At first he was amazed, then he bursted out in laughter. "They won't need streetcars there," he laughed. "You bet your life," I said. "They won't want it there, but I was a motorman on the New York streetcar lines. I was laid off because I only had a temporary contract as a reserve man during the flu epidemic." "Why eh . . . I believe you," he said. "I'm a Freemason," he continued, "I always get work wherever I'd ask for it." "What has freemasonry to do with your job?" I asked. "Well, we always help each other, you see. The Freemasons form a unity for the betterment of humanity and as a consequence the members naturally help each other." "That's about the same with the Knights of Columbus, ain't it?" I said. "Aw, the Knights of Columbus," he said scornfully, "they ain't a unity in the sense of what it is with the Freemasons; they're Roman Catholics and they only fight for their own tribes." He looked, sarcastically smiling, in the direction of the man who sat opposite me. That man reacted almost immediately. "You belong to some tribe?" he asked me, laughing merrily. "By golly, no," I said, "the big idea. I'm a free man. I leave everyone in his own value for the betterment of mankind," I said. The Yankee sat down back in his place when he got aware we poked a little fun with his unlikely story and fell back into silence.

I did not believe he belonged to a Freemason lodge because no member would talk the way he did about the meaning of this society and about its rituals. I had read about all kinds of snug and stylish societies and clubs like the Knights of Columbus, the Odd Fellows, the Elks, the Eagles, the Order of the Moose, and about all sorts of mystical and quasi-mystical societies like the Freemasons and others. It did not interest me at all. But all the same I thought he was a good man.

The man in the corner seat opposite me again addressed me. "I'm Jörgen Dahl, Norwegian." "You told me already," I said. I gave him my name. "I'll call you Jerry," he said with the peculiar Scandinavian tongue in his English pronunciation. "Well, then I'll call you Jörgen; how'd you get to New York?" "I signed off my ship," he said. "That's to say," I remarked, "You jumped ship, didn't you? I did so too." "If you see it that way, well, yes. I did so day before yesterday." "So you've got a job right away," I said. "I'm here quite a bit longer. I was a motorman on the New York streetcar just temporarily. A couple of weeks, then I got fired again. I've now signed on as a laborer at the Bethlehem Steel." "I did so too," Jörgen said, "we are in the same boat." "Hope we'll manage it," I said.

He was dressed well and he had the appearance of one who had done work in an office or a store. Looking closer at him, when he had turned his head, I had a feeling that warned me to be on the alert with him. His eyes had something of slyness.

I did not quite like his face. But, maybe I was wrong. "Well, I'm gonna sleep," I said. "You're quite right," and he also lent back. I soon fell into sleep, luckily, for on arrival in Johnstown next morning at seven o'clock we had to start work at once, rested or not.

It was a gloomy rainy morning. I stood on a hill overlooking the landscape, the dreariness of which was aggravated by the ascending smoke clouds that mixed with smoky fumes hanging over the valley. In the far distance, along the banks of a river, I saw the shafts of coal mines and the glow of red-hot streams of melted iron of blast furnaces. You sure could not sing of this, "How pure is my valley." To the contrary, what I saw was the rough reality of existence. There should be coal, iron, and steel! And there should be gasoline for the cars!

Again I was "hurry upped" through a number of rooms; first the doctor, they seemed not be able to do without him in whatever concern. Everything was all right. Then came the foreman, Bill Willard. He took his pencil and wrote on our enlistment paper the number of our bunkhouse. Our gang consisted of ten men. Seven of them, me included, were directed to bunkhouse number one. Jörgen, the only one I had made acquaintance and had conversed with, was lodged in bunkhouse four. We were allowed ten minutes to take our luggage to the bunkhouses in the camp.

The bunkhouses were big square wooden structures and they looked habitable. Inside, the walls were whitewashed. Near the wall stood a black iron stove, its pipe straight up through the ceiling. A door in the rear gave entrance to the washroom, put up with a number of showers. This washroom lied between two bunkhouses, so it had two doors. Against the walls were on each side twelve bunks, each covered with two blankets which lay over the burlap mattress. Seventeen men were housed there already, the beds of whom were made. We had to make our beds so we could sleep the coming night.

Within, the bunkhouse smelled as if someone had twisted out a wet mop. I sniffed the air to detect the eventual scent of bugs that might be around. It did not smell like if they were there. "No pants rabbits?" the guy, standing before his bunk next to mine asked me. "What d'ye mean with pants rabbits?" I asked. "Let's call 'em gray-backs," he said. "I got you," I retorted, "You mean them stinking bugs; it doesn't smell like if they are here. Looks clean to me."

The Bethlehem Steel Corporation, one of the giants of industry in the U.S.A., having, among others, settlements in the area of Johnstown, Pennsylvania. Standing up hill and looking down the valley in the direction of the Cambria Plant you can see red-hot glowing streaks of molten steel, mine shafts, and refineries. Daffodils and daisies can't thrive here—the fumes and gases would prevent this. It ain't a region for them to get on. Funnels and pipelines, steam and smoke and gloominess is all there is to it. But the workers earn a living.

The man showed me the bunk with my number on it and said, "there was a steelworker here." "Why'd he quit?" I asked him. "It wasn't because of any bugs; no, it wasn't that. Why he just quit because he wanted to go. He did not like guys around him." "Was it the food of the camp?" I asked him. "No, it wasn't that. He did not give any reason. And there was plenty of work. When he went, he just said he wanted to move," the man said.

And he proceeded: "He just said, give me my time one night to do whatever any guy outside the camp wanted to do. Aw, you see there were no women around here. He never came back. They will have been looking for him, for he wasn't paid off."

I lifted the blankets and looked underneath; it was clean. "All right," I said, "I'll take this bunk." I put my things in the box on the wall. I had to hurry back to the meeting place to receive further instructions. We again reported to the foreman who said, "Here's your shovel, you guys go with Jim Cernak."

Jim, who wore a black boatman's cap, directed his gang to the surroundings of the refinery, where we were divided in small groups. "You on the backside of that big scrubber; you begin there digging a ditch. That wide," he spread his arms, "one-foot deep." Now he showed a spade length with his spade. "You," he addressed me, "You begin near that shed over there and dig till you meet him; then we'll see further." To all he yelled, "At half-past twelve you may knock off for lunch at the camp mess; at one-thirty you'll be back here again. At five you are through."

So we had to work from seven in the morning to five in the afternoon with only an hour's break; from this hour we had to deduct nearly a half hour for going to and fro the camp mess. We had, in fact, to work about nine hours at a stretch.

And there I stood shoveling ditches the endless day long at a pay of thirty-eight cents per hour—a wretched job. When I had finished at five, I decided to try and change my job for another. I went to the office of the superintendent, McLaughlin, who eyed me curiously. Without any ceremony I told him I did not want this digging job. "The job you gave me; I'd ask you to put me to work somewhere else, this is no job for me." He muttered something between his teeth, looked into his papers and said: "Well, tomorrow at seven apply to boss Bindle in the lime-mixing plant, forty-three cents an hour. Will that suit you?"

I consented, as I thought it would be at least a better job than digging in the ground all day. Moreover, it gave five cents more pay and I thought it a run of luck. What it was in reality I experienced next day. All day long I stood on the same spot stirring up lime in a big square trough with a long mixing iron, stirring the live long day. I got crazy of it and cursed the filthy pestilential damp I inhaled all the time.

At ten minutes past five I again stood before McLaughlin's desk. "What the hell you want now again . . . (and something that escaped my notice!) he snapped at me and I retorted (and now my vocabulary was no longer as unchastened as before) "I ain't impressed, sir, by your treating me on a job like this, like this lime mixing. D'you think I'd be such a transcendental idiot to keep on with this damn work? I bet you won't find a man to do this hell of a job; well, I won't either. This ain't a job for a white man." I began to use the American slang pretty well already. I neither had any notion of the discrimination that was underlying in my words nor any knowledge that the decency of my language was sadly to seek. "What do you really want?" he shouted. "You are unqualified to any specified job. What background have you got?" "Well," I said, "I've sailed as a wireless operator on board ships, a technical function; I know much about electricity and motors. . . . "

He now became thoughtful, while his blue eyes looked past me. "Well," he said at last, "report to Wallace Stegall, the foreman of the scrubbery." Scrubbers are towers in the by-products plant in which the crude benzol is cleaned and other products are distilled. "Now this job will pay you fifty cents an hour; and don't bother me anymore or I'll put you back to digging ditches for which you are contracted." "Another advance in pay," I thought.

Next morning I reported to Wallace Stegall, a rather young man with an open face. He looked at me kind of conceited, as if he would say another good-for-nothing rotter. His rolled up shirt-sleeves showed me some tattooing on his arms; he obviously had been a sailor, a marine man I guessed. The language he spoke I could not quite follow. It sounded like if he came from the South. In the northeastern states—in New York—they spoke another slang. Later I heard he came from Tennessee. I concluded he must have been a boatswain of the American navy, which had left on his personality the imperturbability that makes these men preeminently suited for responsible and sometimes dangerous duties. He wore a sort of locomotive engineer's hat, a high black one with a slanting peak. It looked as if it was made of silk. He ordered me to do all kinds of errands and stray little jobs outside the engine hall and up and around the scrubbers. The scrubber columns were about 70 to 75 feet high and they got their oil supply from the big pump station. An intricate network of pipelines ran overhead across the refinery site and they had a great number of cocks, valves, and water coolers. The crude oil in its turn was distilled from the coal that came from the collieries in the valley, which also belonged to the Bethlehem Steel Corporation.

I fed my eyes on all things that were around and how things worked. I soon noticed that the heart of the refinery palpitated in the pump station, a clean, gleaming hall fitted with turbine pumps, the newest invention, and tens of meters, dials, and cocks. From this point the different fuels and products were distributed and the orders came to open and close valves in the various areas of the pipeline net.

Sometimes I was ordered by the foreman to climb the high scrubbers to inspect the valves on top. If I did not come down within ten minutes, another man was sent up to see if there was something wrong. There always was a cloud of gas up there. So there always was a chance to get unconscious. Once when I had the nightshift I had to go up in pitch dark.

Whatever work I had to do, it was a whole lot better than my former jobs. On the whole it was easy work and nothing particular happened. In my secret heart, however, I hoped there might some day be an opportunity to get to work inside in the motor hall. I had noticed that the motors, the accessories, and the meters were inspected continually. I also soon got aware that they had an extra man in the day and night shifts to take care of this controlling work and to survey the pressure meters. This man should be very much posted up to his job and be always on the alert. Some scrubbers might get without oil, which could be read from the particular meter dial, and then the boss should be informed at once so as to have a valve opened somewhere.

This man, an Italian, had been called to order the other day by the superintendent when he was caught by Stegall in the act of sleeping, just for a little while. To fall asleep, of course, was strictly forbidden in this branch of work; and if you were not fit enough to do your job, you had to report sick. Since that time the boss had him controlled at intervals. Stegall could not very well fire him, because the man was an experienced hand in this kind of work and it seemed not to be easy to replace him by another qualified man.

My aversion against the life in the laborer's camp gradually increased. It did so the more when I met in the laborer's camp two Dutchmen, who also worked around the refinery, presumably for quite awhile already. At first I did not notice they were Dutch because they spoke English all the time. I found out they came from Holland when some day I overheard them speaking Dutch. As I had not much intercourse with the other inmates of the bunkhouse, I made acquaintance. They were called Slim and Shorty and they seemed inseparable. Together they washed under the shower; they worked on the same job— pipeline maintenance. Together they went to the women. This seemed to be indispensable to them, for they did not cease to brag about their pleasures with their darlings. I knew all about this tall talk; in my sailing time I'd heard a lot of swank about this subject.

What I got most sick of was the way in which they talked about our mutual native country, Holland. In their eyes it was a good-for-nothing country without any prospects whatever; small and crowded with narrow-minded people who ought to come to the States to learn to live! From the beginning of my meeting them I quarreled with them and poked fun at their enforced confinement in this low-graded camp. Anyhow, I turned my back on them. I scarcely went to town, which I did not think very attractive. I could not get in touch with people I could freely talk with and, contrary to many others, I did not like the idea to indulge in relations with "red-bagged" females. The camp life kind of depressed me, so I mostly passed my free time with reading.

One day something happened that changed things completely. I was outside the pump room busy to close a valve cock on one side of a sector, while at the same time Wallace Stegall was active in an adjacent sector, apparently on an emergency case. Looking his way I watched him close a benzol valve of the main supply line with a wrench. Then, all of a sudden, I saw a stream of benzol coming with some force out of the flange of the valve. In a moment it flashed upon me that the valve had broken down, so I left my work and ran to Wallace to help him out. The benzol had flown over him and he seemed at a loss what to do. While I hurried to him I drew a tuft of cotton waste from a cotton case at the wall, pulled the shirt from his shoulders, and wiped the benzol off his body the best I could. Benzol is a dirty, caustic stuff and when it touches your skin it may leave burned spots on it when it stays long on your skin. With the utmost speed we cut out the faulty valve by closing the valve of the adjacent sector with a big wrench; in this way the supply was cut off. With a tearing speed we ran into the shower room to clean his body. He was lucky we cleared it so fast; his skin was only a little irritated.

Next morning I was called by Mr. McLaughlin; who told me he could use men like me in the engine hall and offered me the job of the sleepy Italian. I did not care about what happened to this man. If he did not do his duty the way he ought to, he was apt to get fired. Should it have happened to me, nobody would have cared about me either.

I now got a swell job, compared with the ones I had before. My pay was raised to eighty-three cents an hour. The engine hall had to be kept clean, the meters should be strictly watched, and the thermocouples controlled and regulated. To assist me I had a special man at my disposal. It was continuous duty, with day and night shifts and also on Sundays. I sure took care not to fall asleep and I even sometimes made a double shift.

In spite of my promotion I had to stay in the camp, because I had not paid off. I hated to enter those gates and to take sight of the uniformed camp police. Not that they were unfriendly; they were not. They had to do the job they had signed on for. Their work at the company was to guard the site. Nevertheless, I felt it as an assault on my personal liberty, just like if I was treated as a prisoner—innocently sentenced—waiting for his parole.

I must admit, though, that it was necessary to protect the immense industry some way or the other, but I could not agree with the way it was done. The guards had to be on the alert against sabotage or what may lead to it. They also had to intervene in case of labor disputes or when laborers kicked a row. All individual defiances against the rules could be punished by them; that I did loathe. It was none of their business, I thought. They also were used to break strikes, which might occur on account of lousy labor conditions, bad food, or other unfavorable things. This little private police force had to be maintained by sheer necessity. One must not forget that these gigantic industries contracted armies of workers of different nationalities, which not always could bear each other having different customs and habits. Puerto Ricans hated Mexicans, Serbians were engaged in fisticuffs with Croates. Also political and racial diversities were responsible for incidents. So, Roman-Catholic Irishmen fought Protestant Irishmen, white Yankees scolded black people as "niggers."

The camp police often were called for assistance in order to end brawls of drunks. In the mining districts of Pennsylvania, namely, there was much drunkenness, particularly among the miners. This arose from the fact that as a consequence of the prohibition many miners families illegally distilled their own liquor. This resulted in an increase of drunkenness among the always thirsty miners and laborers.

Unskilled labor was mainly done by immigrants and aliens—people from abroad. The Americans themselves did

Refining coal and oil is a rather new trade. You will have to have the know-how and be kind of cool headed to run these intricate constellations, for pipelines, valves, tanks, and fumes enclose you oppressively. If you can't stand this, you should not go to work there. Once in awhile there's a breakdown; you always have to guard yourself and be on the alert. Undoing the defect is the first requirement to prevent disasters.

not err on it. They did not like heavy work—"coolie labor." The organized craftsmen, closed-shop men, the people who manned the higher jobs, were mainly Anglo-Saxon bred. Like in ancient times highly developed countries made use of "mercenaries" to defend their interests. Today America has its mercenaries to do the unattractive and tiresome labor. To these mercenaries also belong the Negroes. In this area these latter worked for the greater part in the steel mills and were lodged in separate camps. For the second time in my life I became confronted with race discrimination. The first time I had a foretaste of it two years ago in Montreal, when I was in a bar drinking a glass of beer. In an adjacent hall I witnessed white people throwing hard balls with utmost force at the head of a Negro standing behind a curtain, only his head sticking out. His black head skillfully evaded the balls. As far as I could see none of the white guys managed to hit him. I was disgusted to see how the ballpitchers looked at the Negro with pent-up fury.

I guess that Negro probably earned good money with the human unworthy game.

It appeared to me that in Canada at the time as well as in the U.S.A. today, the Negro was still considered to be a low-rate citizen. At present, in the twenties, sixteen percent of the American population consists of Negroes. Much of the bad terms on which many white men were with the black people was contributed to by the Jim Crow acts.

After the liberation of the black slaves the race separation was carried into effect with fast pace. In the beginning this discrimination only referred to the blacks. Later, other races were also involved. With respect to the Negroes, part—and not the best part—of the white Americans did not hesitate to give evidence of their hate in a sinister way.

In the papers I read about the revival of the Ku Klux Klan and of the stirred up agitation against all colored people; and not only against them, but also against Jews and Roman Catholics. The KKK opposed against the "bastardization" of the white race. In their hysterics they did not even shrink from the lynching of Negroes; they hung them on some rigged-up charge. In the deep South, in Alabama, these pursuits were the worst. At the Bethlehem Steel Corporation, here in Pennsylvania, white people were not allowed to enter the camps of the black people and reverse. Several times I had been standing before the closed iron gate looking into the camp trying to have a chat with its residents. The Negroes sure liked to talk to me too, but the camp police gave me to understand that I had to move on. I still hear the blacks sing with their deep voices "Ol' Man River" and I also remember their "Dixieland." Once I heard those steel Negroes sing a typical song, the tune of which I had heard before, the words of which I was never able to understand, however. Much later I finally found out what the words were like, they were:

> John Henry had a li'l woman
> Her name was Polly Ann
> On the day that
> John Henry dropped down dead
> Polly Ann
> Hammered steel like a man.

John Henry must have been a proud Negro and his wife seemed to have been a resolute woman.

The "steel Negroes" as I saw them work in the steel mills of

Johnstown were just as good or bad as any white man in doing their job. I got fed up with the difference of treatment, not only of the Negroes, but also of the unskilled laborers and I longed for the time I should be permitted to leave this undomestic camp. And that was very soon; at the end of the week. Now I'd got the new job I was able to pay off and leave the bunkhouse at last.

Finding a room, however, proved to be very difficult. I told Wallace I was looking for a room, if possible near to the plant, and that I had looked all over the ads in the newspapers without success though. "Why don't you try at Mrs. Cooper's in Chestnut Street; that's quite near to the refinery," he said. "She often has rooms to let and tries to get decent tenants. She's got a big house, too big for a young woman like her. She only takes people on recommendation. Just tell her I've sent you—we know each other. I worked together with her husband. Since he died two years ago—he had a good job here—she's been compelled to let rooms and do some part-time work for a living. Her husband bought the house and left her a mortgage debt to be paid off." I did as Wallace said and called on her next evening. By chance she had a room open and I indeed was accepted as a tenant of a small but comfortable room.

The house of Mrs. Evelyn Cooper, a good-looking woman, a brunette (I estimated her age on 25 to 26), was a rather big house. She looked far too young to be a widow. She sure had have bad luck her husband died so young. I believed that notwithstanding her loveliness she was a plucky woman, the way she managed to keep alive, and I thought she was to the point but not forbidding. Everyone called her Lyn and according to the American custom I too called her by that name. I told her when I applied for the room that Wallace sent me and that she could inquire after me at him. But she said, "Never mind, I can judge for myself. I take you." I thought her very sympathetic and I believed we should get together very well.

"You been to Lyn Cooper?" Wallace asked me next day. "I was there all right and she takes me; thanks for your introduction." "Don't be too sure you'll stay there," Wallace said. "She's a clever woman. She needs the money, but don't fool around her. She ain't that way as far as I know her. Just keep this in mind."

Wallace Stegall and his buddy Don Marshall had their rooms in Graham Street, not far from Mrs. Cooper's house.

Both were single and they each had a girl downtown. I did not quite know, but I had the idea that they had not the same girl all the time.

I liked the job I had. In idle moments I sometimes walked around the scrubbers and watched the men with whom I came from New York to Johnstown. They were still digging ditches and doing labor associated with it; the work had been moved farther away near the Steel Mill. The Norwegian, Jörgen Dahl with whom I got acquainted in the train, since we were here frequently sputtered out his gall about the lousy job and blamed himself from the bottom of his heart that he ever had been foolish enough to change his sailor's job for this darned digging job. I did not agree with him. You could always get work here and if you did your best you could even make promotion. "Look at me," I said, "I've got no shovel anymore. I think America is a fine country and the people are friendly and helpful." I saw him lose his temper and shovel a heap of dirt and throw it away angrily. I could not help he had made no headway.

Jörgen was a sturdy guy, but I wondered hard whether it would be wise to concern myself with him. Looking at his face I had the idea he wasn't quite trustworthy. He was blond and had blue eyes, which crept under his upper eyelids and peered to you from under them. I did not pay much attention to it; we were on friendly terms and I just had to have someone to talk shop and compare myself with. I could pull myself up this way. When I left him, we made the appointment to see each other later in the evening.

For two months I worked with the Bethlehem Steel already as a qualified worker to the satisfaction of the superintendent McLaughlin, the big boss. From my room I looked out on the Conemaugh River streaming through the valley, faintly visible because of the clouds and the vapors of the industries. There were factories all over and far in the distance I saw mine shafts. Still farther, behind the mines, was the big boulder dam with the power station. This dam kept the water on high level, the basins supplying the power for the turbines, which in turn generated the electric power for this region and a great part of the state of Pennsylvania. They began to rebuild this dam after the catastrophe of 1889, when exceptional heavy rains formed a torrent of water roaring from the mountains and overflowing the basins. The abundant surplus of water caused the old dam to burst. The whirling water flood falling down upon the part of Johnstown that lied 30 feet lower destroyed practically all the houses there. More than two thousand people perished in this disaster. A number of factories also were totally dragged away by the water. This happened just about thirty years ago and by this time the dam and all houses, plants, and factories had been rebuilt, the latter two bigger and more efficient with the most modern equipment. The houses were built higher up on the hills.

I earned a good wage now, but I could not save much money because I had to pay quite a lot more for room and board than I had to in the camp. My fellow-lodgers were an elderly man who worked as a timekeeper at the work preparation of the steel plant—his name was George Belling—and a woman of about forty, Maggie Wentworth, who was in charge of the mess of the same plant. Nice people to get along with and with whom I had much conversation. It was the woman who told me I could get my citizen's papers right away if I just got married. I did not go further into this matter, as I considered myself too young. I was twenty-three and I loved my freedom too much then to be lured into matrimony. Maybe she was prompted to this idea by the fact that Lyn and I had been stepping out much of late. I, indeed, went out a good deal—to a party sometimes and to the movies or a music performance and I did not always go alone. I often asked Lyn to go out with me and then we had a good time. However, she remained reserved against possible overtures from my side. Notwithstanding her youth she was not a woman to get easily entangled in love affairs. But the more I learned to know her, the more I longed to be with her; and I had the idea this longing gradually became mutual.

For all that, however, I had the stamp put on me that I was not naturalized. I had no claim on whatever right the American citizens had naturally. I enjoyed going out with the girls, but I had to curb myself. Lyn did not care about my being an alien as such. "It's the human aspect that counts to me," she said. All the same, I became very intimate with her. She was a good sport and a real woman, although the first time she remained cautious under my caresses.

I was more at ease than ever since I stayed in the U.S.A. The regular work I was engaged in and the pleasant surroundings in Lyn's home contributed a whole lot to this. I had the idea sometimes that Maggie eyed me kind of suspicious as if she would say I don't know for sure, but I have my doubts as to his behavior. But Maggie was a woman and with women intuition plays a prominent part. Lyn took care of her boarders without preference to anyone in particular, correctly and friendly, and she gave no occasion to any gossip. As to me, I rather did like the way I lived.

At the office of the Bethlehem Steel they would certainly know my name, like must have been the case at the New York Streetcar Company. If ever there had been an investigation after me, it would have been so after I had left Manhattan, for it would have been an easy trick to trace a motorman. I wondered if any immigration man was to look after me on the balcony of a streetcar. I guess no one would hit on the idea to do so, because illegal immigrants as a rule would hide themselves to all the world and his wife. They would have had come to the conclusion it was like looking for a needle in a haystack to go over all little private labor agencies; looking after me in this way was hardly conceivable. It would not be likely they'd find me here. I felt quite safe here.

All the same, the field of my present activities did not fit in with my background. My former profession had given me a certain independence on a higher level and my restlessness mainly arose from my ambition to reach my former self again. Added to this, my internal unrest sprung from a sort of obsession to wander to unknown horizons—to witness new impressions of human life. Well, let me say it, in my heart I still was an adventurer. But it did not prevent me from doing my job to the best of my ability. And everyone was content with it.

Just when I got firmly adapted to my environment, fate ordained otherwise. On a bad day McLaughlin sent for me. He informed me, as he already had done to others before me, that he had orders to discharge part of his personnel on account of overproduction. The younger men were the first to be laid off. He declared that during the election time—the time proceeding the election of a new president—all economic activities were temporarily stopped and all production retained because no one knew what economic policy the new president would follow. In consequence of this, the industry was impelled to lay off superfluous labor forces. Of the laborers working here only a few were organized in unions and there were no social

Miles of rails over which mankind will
travel in their trains are piled up virgin-
ally in the rail-drawing mills. They are
made of the hardest steel, product of
the Bessemer pear that melts the ore
and gets the steel ready to fabricate all
kinds of things. Many working people
and machines are necessary to run the
mills, which are continuously in action,
for steel is the backbone of Pennsylvania's economy and the world is the
market.

provisions. They were just given the sack on short notice and without further pay. They had to see for themselves in what way they should keep their head above water. And this happened in a country that was considered the richest in the world, a country with a gigantic industrial potential, a country that dominated the world markets. America—that had the biggest gold reserve in the world stored in the safes of Fort Knox, and that had a Wall Street that dictated the money markets of the world.

"Things will be better," McLaughlin said, "as soon as the new president will have announced his State of the Union." In this statement the new president discloses his view on the future and this will determine what trade policy is to be followed. Mac looked kind of optimistic.

With regard to the economical position of the country and of the political constellation, a smart set of power pulls the wires. This power set forms an elite, which mainly originates from the big industries and big business like the trusts. These in turn manipulate their own pressure groups. These latter exert their influence upon whatever subject or instance that may add to their retaining power. They also artificially induce unemployment when it suits their interest to get rid of overproduction or to control wages and prices. If Calvin Coolidge should be elected as a president—and everything pointed that way—the economical situation would soon be better. The industry and all big concerns, however, carefully shirked the boat until the time they should know about how "Silent Cal" would lead the nation. Coolidge should be able to clear away things with the aid of the pressure groups that were on his side. The automobile industry had, in fact, suffered the least of the depression. Henry Ford's gospel—high wages, low prices, and mass production on the running belt—exercised a wholesome influence on the working conditions, the zest to work, and the productivity. The workers had good wages; they were in a position to buy a car themselves, although they paid it on installments. But, what of it! I myself had gotten my job with the Bethlehem Steel on installments.

With respect to the authority of presidents, in connection with the economical situation and as a consequence of it, the policy of a weak president could lead to fraudulent practices. Quite recently a scandal of this kind was brought to light. It was the notorious Teapot-Dome scandal in which a top figure of the government, a friend of the president, was involved. This man, Fall, leased the oil fields of the state to private concerns. It was an example of corruption that could arise from the weak-kneed attitude of the president when he proved to be a man-about-town. The investigation of a Senate's committee revealed the guilt of President Harding, who might have had to resign on account of this, but he died before the disgraceful revelations.

However it may be, the candidacy of Calvin Coolidge for the new presidency at present was the cause of the existing unemployment wave. The unmarried men were the first to get fired. McLaughlin would make an exception for me; he offered me a temporary job as a ditchdigger again. He would see to it later, when further developments had made it possible for him to give me back my old job. I thanked him for his well-meant offer, but rejected it because not for all in the world would I like to dig or to do any low-grade work again.

I had earned enough to get through for awhile and made plans to look for other work. I went to see Jörgen to tell him about my discharge. He, too, was fired together with a number of other young diggers. It looked to me I probably would have gotten his job had I accepted McLaughlin's offer. Jörgen and I were on friendly terms for quite awhile already and we talked about what we should do. "What shall we do, Jörgen; stay here? I'd like this most of all; we could wait awhile for better times." I suggested. "No, I don't want this damned job any longer," he said. "Let's go back to New York."

We pondered about a whole lot of possibilities. "Let's take the train to Cleveland and find a lake boat." "But then we'll be broke before we get there and we got to keep some money in our wallets, anyhow," I said. "Couldn't we better go out West and try to [get a] lift? It saves money," Jörgen put forward. "Just leave Lyn Cooper, she'll be all right." "This has nothing to do with her," I said fretfully, "We are obliged to find work elsewhere. Without a job you are nowhere."

And again the spirit of adventure took possession of me and made everything unsettled. We talked about it and decided to go to California and try and get an engagement with the movies in Hollywood. In what capacity even we did not know ourselves. We'd see to it when we were there. I had to admit we were not so good looking; anyway, we doubted ever to become a superstar. But you never could tell.

I told Lyn about our plans. I perceived doubt in her reactions. She did not agree with my intentions. "It's doing things the haphazard way. You should not venture it that way; why don't you just stay here? I don't mind to care for you," she objected. "I can't do otherwise than to give notice, Lyn. My savings will not be sufficient to hold out very long and I don't like to live at your expense. Please, understand me. I like to have it that way. I hate to leave you, but I have my pride. I can't get the work here I like. They offered me a ditchdiggers job—a job I despised already when I got here. I just have to go to find work somewhere else. I'll be back after awhile when times are better. We'll get together again." She said she did not care much about it; all the same there was grief in her eyes. My leaving her sure did not fall on good ground and I believed she saw it as a disloyalty from my part. But I stuck to my point.

Jörgen and I intended to dress ourselves as well as we could. With part of the money we had earned we bought us a new suit; I got a dark blue, he a brown one. We had decided to go on the hitchhike tour. What was left of our money—I had thirty and Jörgen twenty dollars—would be enough to start with; we had not a care in the world. On the way out West we would see in what manner we would earn some money to keep our cash to the mark. I felt myself too independent to sing it out and stay where I was. Perhaps I was kind of callous by nature. This was obvious, for I, too, had not written to my parents for a long period and I sure must have grieved them by not doing so. But then I was too busy with myself trying to reserve my rights of self-determination to bother much about it. Besides, I was too young to realize I might be hurting others by it; my adventurous spirit seemed to prevail over all other things. Anyway, I just wanted to get away.

Actuated by our good intentions, we had determined to leave Johnstown next morning, to be exact, on October 10, 1923, going on our way to Hollywood, the Mecca of all youngsters dreaming of fame. We would hide our dollar bills under the innersoles in our shoes. No thief would hit upon the idea to look for loot there. The evening before, I had said goodbye to Wallace and Don. Early in the morning the following day, I took leave of my housemates.

I hugged Lyn tenderly and kissed her goodbye.

On the Road

OUR FIRST ROUTE would take us to Blairsville. We followed the highway outside Johnstown and walked along the banks of Conemaugh River. We stopped at what we thought was a convenient place along the road to try and get a lift from some motorist. Trying to get a lift meant that you had no money or, as was the case with us, that you could not get to it! Did they know we had our cash in our shoes?

A car stopped to take us in. It was a farmer going to western Pennsylvania. "You feller's broke?" he asked. "Yeah, kind of a depression now," I said. "Got fired," Jörgen added. "They had no more work for us; we'll try to find it elsewhere," he continued. "Quite right, you can't do without," the farmer said after awhile.

First we rode through the spur of the Appalachian Mountains and gradually came into undulating farmland, variegated by woodlands. "We've just gone off the Forbes Road," the man said. We had driven about an hour on this quite busy road. In Pleasant Hills we reached the right bank of the Ohio River. "Now we're coming on the Cumberland Road. It's a kind of a highway that leads to the West," he again said, breaking the silence. Near the place Fredericktown he turned South. We had to step out because we intended to go in the direction of Cleveland on Lake Erie. We thanked him for his hospitality and parted with a handshake.

We proceeded our way through farmland, being many miles away from Johnstown already. We walked a couple of hours till we reached Little Beaver Creek where we were deep into the state of Ohio. We had the luck to get another lift and drove via Freeburg and Greentown to a number of lakes—the Willodale and the Portage lakes. After we got out and said goodbye to our friendly transporter, we walked further along the Erie Canal in the direction of Cleveland.

Jörgen and I were not quite used to each other. At first we

could not very well fit in the way of travelling together. We each had our own sphere of thinking. I knew him only from the train trip from New York to Johnstown and from our stay in the camp. He was in another bunkhouse than I; his number was four, my bunkhouse was number one. In the camps the mutual relation between the laborers was one of self-preservation. Everybody cared for his own business and nobody else had to meddle in it. You had to prove yourself. On a journey like this you, too, had to prove yourself. Jörgen's attitude I thought was somewhat unmannered. From the beginning when I got to know him, he had acted on me as something of a spiritual screw jack on which I pulled myself up. I had found out that the intimate relations between men and women seemed to haunt him like the scraps a dog was longing for all day long; it may finally get it or not—it all depended upon what sort of a dog it was. I did not know, a sneaky one or a decent one. I could not gauge his character.

I was awakened from my thoughts and also Jörgen stirred when the noise of a motorcar became louder and louder. When the car approached us, we put up our thumbs in the habitual manner. The driver was a farmer from western Pennsylvania who was on his way to Mansfield. He took us only a few miles west. Having walked again for a couple of hours, we had the luck a family with a big car stopped to take us in. In this Chevrolet sedan there was but little room on account of the big family that was packed in it. There was a father, a mother, and two sons, who moved up so we could sit, though with some effort. We had no luggage, for we lived by the day.

So far, all Americans I had met had been very kind to me, even in "inhuman" New York. Giving us a lift caused these people much inconvenience, but this family seemed to feel it their duty to help us out. Here again I met with the kindheartedness of the American people. The idea that we were in low water urged them to help us. It was not that bad with us. They could not be conscious of our hiding our money between the inner soles of our shoes. And naturally we did not tell them. Our conversation proved to be very interesting, especially when it came to the old country. To most Americans the word old country causes some nostalgia, for many American families descend from the peoples of Europe.

They let us down a few miles before Cleveland where they had to turn to the left on their way to southern Illinois. We had to walk for more than an hour to reach town. We followed

Detroit Avenue, which ran parallel to the shore of Lake Erie. In this neighborhood the offices of the Lake Steamship Companies were situated. I believed we were near 60th Street, but I am not quite sure of that. The first thing we did was to inquire at the offices of the shipping master whether there might be a chance to get engaged on board of some lake boat. These lake boats were long ships, especially built for the heave of the lake water; they were not seaworthy and would probably break in two should they venture to sail on the high seas. They were only suited to sail the Great Lakes between Chicago and the Saint Lawrence River.

If we might have the luck to get a ship job, Hollywood would have to wait awhile for its future "stars." There were long rows of applicants—"mermen" we called them—waiting for their turn to be called inside. Those long rows made it impossible for us to entertain at least a little hope ever to sail on the Great Lakes or to get a job as a longshoreman. After all it was a good thing, for we were not in the possession of legal papers and on second thought we could not permit ourselves to be so reckless to accept a higher grade job. We had to confine ourselves to jobs for which no papers were required, and these jobs did not grow on the bushes.

We turned our steps downtown to find a sleeping place for the coming night and to take a bath and wash our shirts. We found a boardinghouse in the harbor quarter. Then we went to find a barbershop to have a shave. We had a good night's sleep and a substantial breakfast and soon we walked to the highway again for a possible lift. Having waited for a new lift endlessly, a friendly woman stopped to take us—poor wretches—in her car. The United States of America was a progressive country and the emancipation of the women had obviously advanced that much that they would even be allowed to drive a car all by themselves. She had our company till about ten miles from Toledo and again we waited a long time before someone would be so kind to take us into the city.

Lifting proved to be not as easy as we had supposed it would be. After all, on closer reflection, it was a manner of begging. You profited from the willingess of the motorist to offer you part of his or her car room without any charge. We walked further and passed Lemoyne. At last we reached Toledo. We looked around to see how labor conditions were here. We did not understand what was up. The whole nation apparently seemed to be awaiting what the White House was to decide for their good when the new president was elected. We applied for work wherever we thought there might be a possibility to succeed. We booked no results. After a few days searching for a job and staying in the hotel, our dollar stock began to dwindle slowly but surely. There was nothing else to it than to go out West as fast as possible to the vast farm area west of the Mississippi to what they called the Middle West. There we sure would find work.

To save our money and to travel fast we decided to ride the freight trains, if need be, between the wheels. We took our bearings to the railroad yards to feel our way, for we were quite unknown with the art of jumping on trains. I had found out that the trains of the Union Pacific and the Chicago North Western went West to the Middle- and Northwestern states. The construction in earlier days of the Union Pacific Railroad in particular, ushered in a new era and put an end to the mail coach and the pony express. This earliest of railroads to the West for the most part carried the old pioneers, who trailed from the East to the western farmlands. These pioneers were for the greater part Scandinavian, Swiss, Dutch, and German immigrants who mainly settled in Michigan, Illinois, Iowa, and the Dakotas. Those who went further West were the gold seekers and adventurers. In the newspapers I had read how many railroads there were in the U.S.A. Beside the Chicago North Western there were other railroads that went out West: the Chicago Great Western, the Pacific, and the Pennsylvania Railroad. I afterwards came to the conclusion that America had the most railroad companies of the world. To mention a number of them: the Baltimore and Ohio, the Marquette, the Illinois Central, the Michigan Central, the Chesapeake and Ohio, the New York Central, the Rock Island and Nickleplate, the Chicago, Burlington and Quincy, the Chicago, Milwaukee and St. Paul, the Southern Pacific, the Grand Trunk, etc.

We were sharply attentive to what rails the trains were switched on. The Baltimore and Ohio trains, too, made use of these tracks, but those trains were of no use to us. They went in another direction and operated in the eastern states. The Chicago and North Western trains tracked the old Indian routes to the far West, the route we planned to follow at least till we reached Chicago. From there we could try to catch the Santa Fe that went to Southern California. We figured out all these things—the route to California ran via Colorado and Arizona. Well, we'd see to that later. In our secret heart we wondered if we should ever manage to get out there.

It looked to us that it would be quite hard to jump on a riding train the way experienced tramps did. Not so long ago three of them were killed under the wheels because they missed the handles. You must catch hold of handles or any other protruding iron you got sight of and keep it tight. To ride between the wheels—behind the buffers—you must crawl under a standing train and you got to do it quickly before someone of the personnel sees you.

We waited till the darkness to start with our operation and ventured to hide somewhere along the tracks of the switching yard so we could see approaching trains from which we might assume they would go West. The spot under a viaduct we considered most suited for our purpose; our field of vision covered the greater part of the yards. We were looking over a multitude of rails projecting in a western direction and which were quite near to our hiding place. Every time a shunting locomotive rode towards us it threw the fierce sheen of its headlights under the viaduct and illuminated the place we were seated. And every time we thought, this must be our chance. And then when the opportunity did offer itself, all of a sudden two men jumped down before us. In their hands they carried a gun and a flashlight and they shouted: "All right, you guys, come out o' there. What's the big idea, what dy'e do out there? Come out quickly or we use our guns." We came out, not quite scared, for in our subconsciousness we were prepared for such incidents. At least I was. As to Jörgen, I wasn't quite sure of him. He tried to save face and made himself ready to go in the defense. I kicked him against his shins to pull him up. These guys were railroad policemen; these men were engaged by the companies to guard the yards and the trains and to watch against thefts. They also had the authority to take delinquents into custody. Again I prod Jörgen in the ribs to bring him to his senses. We were no match against these fellows. Luckily he drew in his horns in time.

They searched us for weapons, which we did not have in our possession, and in the mean time I honestly told them what was the matter with us. Our appearance was not that of tramps and we spoke reasonable English, which seemed to make some impression upon the elder of the two detectives. "All right," he said, "you may go, but never try to go hanging on a train so near to the yards; you'll never succeed. We don't care a bit about your having a free ride if you get your chance—till you're thrown off again, but that's not our business. Let's give you some good advice. If you want to get a freight, then just try it on the west side of Toledo city, a few miles past the next viaduct on the other side of the town. You must wait for the train at junction 13. The trains slow down there, so you may have the chance to board one. Well, now beat it, Good luck!"

It was a dark evening and in the blackness of the night it was hard to find the way. We stayed as near to the railroad tracks as was possible. On the west side of the town we at last found something that looked to us like a junction—it was near Springfield. Presumably the detectives had meant this spot. When we arrived there a train, slowly puffing, just banged away over a level crossing. Meanwhile, it had become two o'clock in the night. We now had to wait for our chance. The shining rails were the only visible objects in the deep darkness. Tired to death and having hours ahead before perhaps a train would come, we sat down near the rails, supporting ourselves with tree branches that lay around. We rested, but anyhow, kept awake.

Jörgen was bigger than I, nearly a head, and also stronger; but he was not the brightest. That had become evident the time we were together. On our hitchhike trip he had time and again made efforts to stop in some town for awhile to have the opportunity to get in touch with the girls. I could imagine how he felt. I, myself, would sure like to caress a woman too. At present, however, we just had to abstain from any contact with the fair sex and not to lose sight of what we aimed to do. I made it plain to him that we in our situation could not afford to go into petting parties. "You'd have lost all liking for it if you'd got in trouble. They must not find fault with us. So behave yourself till you are in a position to go your own way freely," I told him. "We can't afford to be saddled with something undesirable." "You got your deal all right; I've done nothing but shovelling and sleeping in those damned bunkhouses," he snapped at me. "Aw, shut up, you sucker," I shouted, "you've got no brains; you're dumb. We ain't got money enough—we're nearly strapped. Now, quit your lap-doodle." I seemed to have eliminated most of his arguments. "You're a monk," he shouted. "Very funny!" I said.

It was a pity we had to fool around in our relatively new

suits for which we had paid so much money. We had to sit on the cold, wet ground, near the bushes that grew alongside the railroad. The brushwood at least kept the chilly wind from blowing through our clothes. We were tired to death. How many miles we had walked that day we did not know. I had a feeling of desperation and I asked myself, like Jörgen also had done before me lots of times, whether I might not have gone the wrong way and would it not be better to have stayed on board ship in New York. It had appeared it would be hard to find work at present. It was of no use, however, to think about this. I had burnt my ships behind me. I could not get back, even if I wanted to. I had to make the best of it. After all, when I pondered about it, my stay in New York in itself had been quite an adventure and also my work in Johnstown had showed me I was capable of finding my way all right. I regained my self-confidence after a while. "I am going to add a new chapter to it," I reflected.

Sleep did not come because we had to keep on the alert. If a train should approach, we should have to be prepared. True to nature the twilight drew near; it gave new hope to us. Once there must come a train. Nature also had its obligations as to our bodily requirements—what had to be done must be done and it had to be done now! In turn we pull a number of sheets off the toilet-paper roll; Jörgen had appropriated the paper from the camp toilets and he carries it in his coatpocket. We disappear behind the bushes. And then, while I am sitting squatted down, I hear the train; the sound of its whistle piercing the stillness of the early morning . . . boooehhh, booehhh, . . . booeh, booeh! "By golly, my pants, there's the train, . . . gosh, hurry-up, I got to get 'em!" Speeding up the posterior after treatment, I tried to pull up my pants, mean-while stumbling to the tracks. Those darned pants won't come up. I see Jörgen frantically waving his arms, "Hurry-up, there he is, hurry-up." Irritably slow the train approaches; its slowness is even too fast now I am trying to reach the track. I get there in time. Where shall we catch it and how! We might miss our hold and trip over—it is a risky thing for us greenhorns. We must not think about it. Once we have taken hold of something we should not let go, for this might be fatal. Booehhh . . . booehhh . . . booeh, booeh!

It really looks like a train of the Chicago North Western. This train will go to Chicago and further on to Minnesota. But then, from Chicago, how should we go further? I don't know; never mind, we'll see to that later. These thoughts are playing through my mind while I am waiting.

The weather is reasonably clear. We can see clearly the contours of the train when it is in the bend. It is composed of a number of low open wagons, covered with a brown tarpaulin and other, higher ones, and also of some tank wagons. The big locomotive, puffing black smoke produced by the brown coal it burns, has drawn near till about 80 feet. We discover various protruding things, which look like handles. We are not sure whether we can grasp them. We also see some iron steps reaching to the roof. We shall have to catch one of these things sticking out on the low wagons and swing ourselves into them someway. I am standing about 30 feet from Jörgen. The locomotive snorts past us and we feel the air displacement. The train moves faster than we had expected—too fast. We have to be careful and keep tight whatever we get hold of. We are aiming with our eyes. Shall we . . . now? Nothing happens. There is no chance of my catching hold of anything. When I

Those who'd like to get off because the country suits them have to watch how and when to jump. Some of them quit jumping for good and stay and settle down in the region they got off because the work and the people suit them. They may become good farmers and may marry a pretty farm girl. Most of them, however, go on being a hobo for years and years till they grow old and can't jump anymore. A lot of them die in the poorhouse. Others disappear in the multitudes.

glance sideways at Jörgen I see him try to grasp a handle. He fails and falls back. In an instant I see him push himself off with his hands and while he is falling I see him turn around his axis. With lightning speed he luckily lands in the sand beside the rails. Terrified, I fail to catch hold of an oncoming handle. I won't risk it now I have seen Jörgen did not manage it; besides, I can't leave him alone. All this happens in a few seconds. Jörgen isn't hurt; he is a tough guy.

This train rides too fast for inexperienced hobos like us. I think those railroad dicks must have known about it; they just kidded us or maybe they really thought us capable of it. The spot we are at this moment does not at all look like a junction. No water loader for the locomotive; the train did not stop, so we could have figured out this could never have been a junction. We mustn't have been on the right spot. Anyway, we had not managed to jump on a train. Perhaps we won't ever be able to catch one. If they all move like this one, they will all be too fast for us. Discouraged, we follow with our eyes the lousy train. Its booehhh . . . , booehhh . . . , booehs sound irritatingly in our

ears when it disappears in the distance. Walking again is all there is to it and we'd have to venture how we'd hit upon a traffic road again so we might get another lift.

We sure haven't made much headway so far and still are only a few miles from Toledo on our way to Chicago. A farmer gives us a lift. He apologizes on our question, saying that he has no work for us. "I can't afford more than the two farm-hands I already have," he says. We are riding on a quiet country road, tree bordered with fenced fields and curious looking cows. On our way we had met in Ohio a whole lot of friendly people, open hearted like most Americans and talkative. It occurred to me that in every new state we travelled, speech was different. In New York, Pennsylvania, Michigan, and Ohio I heard many variations of usage. The farmer puts us off at Sturgis. He turns to the right and disappears on a narrow country road that leads to some faraway farms.

Our cash is dwindling fastly. I've got a few dollars left, and Jörgen's cash is quite to the bottom. Jörgen proposes that he tries to play poker in some joint to make up for our shortage of money. "I'm a good hand at bluff poker," he said. "Look at my face. You see through me? You see what I'm thinking? Why, you don't, and in the poker game your opponents just have to guess what you're playing at. I'm darned good at that." "The other guys may be as good as you, even better," I said. "I'm gonna try it anyhow," he said. "All right," I answered, "if you just quit when it is our time to go further; otherwise, we'd never get out West."

Sturgis looked to us to be a Swedish settlement. At least we thought it was as we saw a number of Swedish signs. We badly needed a shave and therefore decided to go to a barbershop. There we might find out whether there was an opportunity somewhere to play a game of poker. At the barber's there sure would be someone who could inform us about it. We entered a barbershop with a Swedish name on its window— John Mattheson. We got seated and waited for our turn. We sat next to a couple of guys who looked to us as though they might be posted up to what was going on in town. The man beside me had the outward signs of a boozer. His face was reddish and his nose purple. "Are there any speakeasies about here?" I opened the conversation. The man waited a few minutes before he answered. Meanwhile, I went on, "We'd like to have a good drink before going further on our way." It proved to be a good hit. "Well, if you guys so badly need a drink, I can take you to a speakeasy. I wait till you're shaved. I'd like a good whisky myself," he finally answered. "There, too is a gambling joint connected with it, behind the bar door. If you'd like to play a game of cards," he continued after a short pause, "there ain't no cops coming around." Fortune favored us; we had success right away.

Having been shaved, we went to the address at the end of the Main Street. It was a drugstore where one could buy ice cream and milk shakes. The proprietor, hanging over his counter, glanced significantly at the man who was with us. "Can we have a drink?" I asked. "We've got gingerale, a bullpup . . . ," he said. "We mean, you got anything to drink," Jörgen said. "Just a drink, you know!" I added. "What are you looking at?" Jörgen went on. "Nothing; the man who's with you," the man behind the counter said. "He's the boss," the man who came with us whispered. We now asked for a whisky point-blank. The "boss" opened a door and let us into a room where we could get our drinks. We offered Pete a drink, too.

Pete, the man who took us there, whispered some words into the ears of the boss; we could not hear what he said. But another door was opened and we were allowed to enter another room where a number of men were playing cards. There was a place open at one of the tables and Jörgen joined a company of men playing, as he said, "stud poker." Jörgen and I had agreed that he should quit—for some reason he himself should have to find out—at the best moment when he stood on ten dollars profit. It occurred to me, however, that it would not be easy for him to withdraw from the game just when the opposite party was on the losing hand. Besides, we had to buy a couple of drinks, for this was part of the business. It was moonshine, so we had to watch ourselves; we must not get ourselves in trouble. "Remember," I whispered, "if things become quarrelsome, we take to our heels. No mixing up in a row."

We knew which door we had to take to get out if it might be necessary. We had taken good notice of the situation. I came into conversation with a fellow, an old man, who stood beside me with a glass of booze in his hand watching the games. Once in awhile he nipped at his glass and then started to chew on the swallow. I did not perceive whether he did so because he found the stuff that tasty he extended his enjoying it as long as possible, or it was that bad he did not like to get it into his throat right away because he tried to make the most of it. Surely this stuff could not bear a comparision with our good Dutch liquor, famous all over the world as the old Schiedam gin. I told him about the old country and he in turn related about how things were in the United States at present. He seemed to be kind of old fashioned. He did not agree with what he called the brutalization of the poker game. He especially had a grudge against the way they played poker in the big cities like New York, Chicago, and San Francisco (Frisco he called it). Common poker had been degenerated to "strip-poker." In strip poker it gradually had become the practice to make the prearrangement that when the stakes of a lost game could not be paid in cash, they should be compensated by an article of dress, rated at its estimated value. It also could be staked down directly. When strip poker was played by men and women combined and they lost their clothes in this manner, the end might show a lustful scene. And it was not only strip poker the man was offended with, but also that stupid game of Mah Jong, a rage that had come from the "Chinks"—as he put it— of the Far East and which often caused a row. And what about the women? "The women wear the pants and sit upon the men and they won't even care to smuggle this lousy whisky under their petticoats and do a busy trade with it. And they, too, have their kids do some kind of work to get as much money for themselves as they like. So the men're getting idle and finally kick a row because they ran aground while high society steals like a magpie."

"No," he said, "these United States of ours are growing wilder by the day. 'Gay Twenties' they call it—don't let me laugh—dirtyness, moon bathing (nude petting parties in the night), girls taking up with guys in their cars. No, just let me play a common game of poker, that's natural! The rest . . . they can keep it!" He looked kind of melancholic at me and then all at once, turning away, shouted to one of the guys, "You stupid, the nell is in it." Jörgen was deeply concentrated on his stud poker. Stud poker is played with one card down on the table and four cards up in the hand. He had told me that he played poker in all kinds of situations, at home and abroad, on board ships, and in gambling dens. "Everywhere," he said, "I'm a crack in it and I can play it in the American way as well." He sat down at a table with three sturdy guys. I heard them call him a "piker," because he made only small stakes. But they sure had respect for his way of dealing the cards; he dealt them fastest of all. When he was on the winning hand, he raised the bettor one time and he did everything so well that he already had won more than ten dollars. I signalled him, but he did not pay attention to it. The game had taken possession of him. He just could not quit the moment he was winning. I knew he was bluffing all the time. I saw his face. He indeed had a poker face. When he suspected one of the others of bluffing too, Jörgen called his hand and most of the time he exposed the other's bluff.

I frantically tried to call his attention. We had to go now; he had the ten bucks. I was not much of a card player. I often could not follow his moves. I looked at the way he stacked the cards and the speed with which he shuffled. This, however, was the only thing I admired him for. I thought it typical that a man who excelled in playing cards, on one hand, was anything but smart in other aspects, on the other hand. In whatever situation he was, I summoned him to quit playing, otherwise I'd just go alone and leave him to his card friends. "We just have to go," I told the other guys, "we needed the ten bucks and now we shall have to leave; work's waiting for us," I lied. "You won't get the jackpot," I shouted to Jörgen and left the room, banging the door behind me. A moment later I heard some commotion behind me and saw Jörgen running hastily to the outside. It looked to me he had done something that didn't seem to have been appreciated. A truck, by chance, came moving past and we jumped on it. It moved us a good many miles from Sturgis in the direction of Elkhart, crossing the St. Joseph River.

Since our money stock had received a new supply from the poker game, we could breathe more freely. To reach South Chicago we had to cover some 200 miles. Riding a train was out of the question at present because the railroad was tens of miles away from the highway we were on. We were lucky to get a lift for a couple of hours in the right direction. Half an hour later we again got a lift by a fast-driving motorist, speeding us up to reaching the Windy City. Then luck was with us again—it was a farmer heading for the stockyards of Chicago. He took us with him till we reached Racine Avenue. He there had to turn to Cicero, where he had to do some errands. From the place he let us down, we took the "El" to Dearborn Street. In this street, the farmer had told us, were a lot of little hotels and boarding-houses.

It was not as easy as we thought it would be to find a cheap hotel and finally we happened to get two small one bedrooms in the YMCA building in South La Salle Street. We had to pay just one dollar a person for room and breakfast. This was reasonable and the rooms were nice and clean. The following day we did not take the time to look around in Chicago and left the big city from Cicero in the West Side. It took us much time to get to the outskirts.

Next place we headed for was Aurora. We walked all day along a secondary road and passed the night in a little hotel in Earlville, where we had a good wash and an excesssive breakfast—we had the means to pay for it. Far to the west—more than 200 miles, we had to cross the Mississippi to reach the big farm areas. Lifts held off; a few cars were overcrowded so they could not take us in. There was no intensive traffic on these country roads and at the end of the day—it was already getting dark—we were again confronted with the alternative of stopping at a hotel, which would cost us money, or to go further and try to sleep in a barn of a farm somewhere along the road. We decided on the latter.

Illinois was all level farmland, very monotonous. Once in awhile we hit upon a hamlet of farmhouses surrounded with trees and bushes. As far as the eyes reached the landscape was yellowish colored by the cornstalks. Although we aimed at Iowa, the big farmland across the Mississippi, we gave serious consideration to the idea to stop and stay here and ask for work. Most farmers, however, were already provided with help. We thought it better to go further to the West.

Asking for shelter on the farms here proved to be hard. The farmers were kind of stiff when they saw us; we did not understand why. They looked askance at our neat suits. We did not look like farmhands or perhaps they did not trust our appearance somehow. It was getting late. We approached a big grain farm and tired to death we decided to get into the grain shed that stood on some distance from the farmhouse. They apparently did not keep a dog; at least we did not hear any barking. If indeed there was a dog, it would have observed us long before we had entered the yard. It was pitch dark and the farmers family must have gone to bed for quite awhile already and been in a deep sleep.

We plucked up courage and opened the barn. When we were used to the dark we saw and felt a number of oats bins;

square boxes surrounded by long boards that kept the oats from gliding out. In these bins the new crop had been deposited. We each dug ourselves in a bin into the dry, needlelike stuff and tried to sleep. But the oats were chilly and made us shiver. Once in awhile we heard some rustle. Maybe it was done by rats and if there is any animal I do hate then it sure is the gruesome rat. They obviously were eating the belly full of the superfluous supply.

After a while I heard Jörgen in his bin saying, "We're sleeping all right, aren't we?" "Sure, we'll sleep all right," I said. "Good night then, Jerry," Jörgen said. "Good night, Jörgen." There was a quiet for some time. Then Jörgen said, "Can't you sleep?" "No, I can't," I said. "I can't sleep either." "What's the matter?" "Don't know; this bin's all right." "This bin's all right too." "Thinking of Lyn, aren't you?" Jörgen tried. "You're a bright boy," I said.

I began reflecting by myself. I was always close with women who were a little older than me. Why? I thought. More practice, I guess. "Let's have a smoke, old bragger," I went on after awhile. We lit a cigarette. "You hear those damn rats, do you?" Jörgen said. "I hear them, I don't like 'em." "I hate 'em, I get nervous of them." "Be quiet," I said, "did I hear someone walking around?" We stopped talking and listened intensively. "No, it's those damn rats." We threw away our cigarette stumps, taking care we had them out. We tried to sleep, listening to the gnawing of the rats. I got in a doze. She's as cute as cotton, I dreamt. I was awake again.

No, we did not sleep that night and early in the still morning, my watch indicated five o'clock, the farmer already came rumbling between his tools in the shed next to the barn. He probably was not aware of our being in the vicinity—in his particular oats bins. When he had gone, we rapidly moved out of our sleeping place and made our getaway, having the luck nobody saw us. Much later we learned that sleeping in a barn like we had done was quite usual and that the farmers, in spite of their surly aspect, were not at all so inhospitable as they had looked like to us. If we should have pressed our point, they would sure have taken us in. But we did not know this at that time and considered their stiffness to be a refusal. Actually, we sneaked past the dead wall of the stable and reached the road again without having been noticed. Jörgen, who, after all, was not in a festive state of mind because of the failure with the train, scolded all that had to do with farming. I gave his mood the free run. I was convinced I'd leave him to his own some day. I could not quite get on with him; he had a rude mentality that I could not always appreciate. We stayed together because we were in the same boat.

We walked on a country road, which might lead us to a highway or at least to a road with traffic. It was early in the morning, half past five, when we approached another farm lying on the right side of the road. At the entrance of the farmyard, a big black dog was watching us coming his way. He did not bark and at a distance it looked like a mean dog. We hesitated; what'd we do? We couldn't get back without losing face to the beast. We just had to go on. We clenched our teeth and walked further. "Let's step on firmly," I said softly, though I had my doubts. The dog still remained silent; it did not make any movement. Mindful of the saying "barking dogs seldom bite," I expected some mischief. Walking undauntedly and looking indifferently—but perhaps the dog felt our fear—we nevertheless went on. And then we passed him; he did not do a thing. We sighed with relief, for it was a bear of a dog.

When we were about five miles past the little town of Dixon, a car caught up with us and as usual we stuck up our thumbs. The driver stopped and we hopped in. The car was a brand new Chevrolet that seemingly had come straight from the transport belt, maybe just a few days ago. The driver, David Blackwell, was breaking in this new car type. He was engaged with the Chevrolet plant in Detroit. His route ran via Clinton to the south of Kansas and back to the factory. He had to cover a fixed number of miles so as to be able to test the behavior of the car under all kinds of circumstances and weather conditions between a certain time limit. He was only too glad to take us with him. He drove alone all day long and was eager to have some conversation "with people he could talk sense with," he said. He listened with great interest to our relating about the old country and he seemed to be quite impressed about our knowledge of the American language and the entertaining manner in which we expressed our thoughts into words.

In order to reach Clinton, we had to pass the bridge across the Mississippi. Toll money was levied there, amounting to a dime. Only car drivers had to pay this toll when they wanted to cross the bridge. With a generous gesture I produced a dime from the scanty stock in my wallet, under protest of David, who said that the factory paid all of his expenses. I thought it was the least we could do to pay for his kindness to take us along so many miles.

From Clinton we drove to Cedar Rapids, where he had to follow another road. We thanked David for the mighty fine ride we had with him. If his friendly words about our native countries might come through, we "bright young men certainly would make it in the States," as he expressed it. He hoped once to hear from us, anyway. With a firm handshake, we parted.

And there we stood, in the heart of the Middle West, in the well-known Quaker Oats town, you know—"the fastest way to a warm breakfast, eat H.O.!" We saw the gigantic factory in the distance.

Our financial state was below zero; we had exceeded our budget quite a bit and we had to have a job now, whatever one it might be, to earn some dough. Our application for work at the Quaker Oats turned out negatively. The situation was getting grave. Our wallets were practically empty and we did not very well like the idea of drifting into an obscure night asylum for bums. The only thing that occurred to us was to take our suits to the pawnbroker to get some money and dress a little more simple. It was a sad idea, but we had to. The pawnbroker only gave us five dollars for each suit, together with khaki pants and a shirt for each of us. "Gratuitously," he said. We were allowed to change dress in a back room. Outside again we roared with laughter—we looked like phoney cowboys who had lost their hats in a saloon fight, for a hat had not been included in the bargain.

We had all afternoon to look for work. Sauntering from one place to the other, we got sight of a little, plain hotel and booked a room for the night, beforehand. The hotelkeeper, if I may use this stately name, was a Bohemian—John Pilnick was his name. He proved to be a kind man who gave us all kinds of hints how to obtain a job. "You fellah's might go look around the station," and he added, "If you'd like to jump on a westbound freight, well, tomorrow there comes a couple of hobos who'll stay in my hotel. Day after tomorrow they'll take a freight to the Middle West; there's lots of work. They'll try to go there and get work as a hired man. Most of 'em are corn pickers. They come here every year in the late fall. They know how to tackle the job on the freight train. Maybe you guys can join them if you'd like to and have the heart to do so," he said.

We went out in search of a job. Having walked around the station and along the railroad shacks we just intended to turn our backs to it when on my right side my eyes fell upon a railroad wagon loaded with coal and standing on a sidetrack near to a warehouse. A few yards above the wagon we saw an open hatch, probably meant for the coal to be shovelled into. We went to the loading clerk of the railroad station to ask him whether we could earn some money by unloading the wagon. "Sure," he said, "if you'd like to shovel it empty, you may do the job. We'll pay you guys fifteen dollars to clear it. "All right, we take the job," Jörgen said. "Agreed," I said, too, although I thought it a hunger pay. Forty tons of coal! Softheaded guys we were! We had to pitch it 5 feet high into the small square hole above us.

"We should have asked for more pay," I said to Jörgen. It took us all afternoon to unload the wagon. With a big sweep of the shovel we had to throw the coal exactly into the little black hole. In the black of the coal dust we toiled till the job was done. Those fifteen dollars were well earned. When we got back in the hotel a couple of men unknown to us, gaped at us. The hotel manager smiled with appreciation. "You guys 've made it, I see. It must've cost you a lot of sweat," he laughed. "I told them fellars here, who'll jump the train tomorrow, you'd like to join them, wouldn't you?" he proceeded.

Having washed and freshened up ourselves, we entered the dining room and joined a group of guys whom we had not seen before. They must be those corn pickers. They were sitting around the table, waiting for their meal, and talked about the course of things and where they should go and how. Usually, in this time of the year, they aimed at the Mid West farms to help getting in the crops, particularly the corn crops. They would earn a good deal of money by going from one farm to the other. The men looked like hobos. Three of them were Yankees, two German, one Irish, and, if we should join, one Norwegian and one Dutchman—in total, eight men. Our linking up with the gang seemed to have been automatically accepted and it gave us a voice in the plan. With a majority of votes it was decided that we should leave next morning at six o'clock and go to the switch yard where all trains departed in a slow tempo.

It was October and the weather was rather chilly. We had to

buy some more clothes to protect ourselves against the cold in the time coming. We also had to buy new shoes. At the barber's we had a haircut and a shave. Having paid for room and board, we had spent more than the fifteen bucks. We should be careful with spending.

Harvest time would soon be there and therefore we should be near to the Corn Belt to be ready to start whenever we may have gotten hired. The month of November, when all corn-stalks were shrivelled to a dry yellow state, is the best corn-picking time. Then the corn ears would hang heavily on the stalks and it would be relatively easy to handle them. That time was for the corn pickers on tour the best chance to apply for work at the farmers. This way of making money accounted for the great number of wandering unemployed—the hobos—who rode the freight trains this time of the year. This manner of travelling saved them a lot of money and if they were lucky to find work for the whole season, they might earn enough money to be able to live through the rest of the winter.

Again we hear the booehh-booehh . . . booeh, booeh . . . of a train. The leader of our little gang—there is always a leader—a tawny, dark-haired American, gives us to understand the time has come to get in action and he shows us how to jump on a train as safely as possible. He sticks out his hands, the right one upwards, the left one down, his right leg sideways to the right as far as possible. "This is the jumping position," he says. The left leg serves as a balancing weight. He gazes at an approaching train. "It's the Santa Fe," he yells, "they are freights and tankers; fine to ride on. Beware of too far protruding ends; let those go, just catch hold of the handles—they're safe," he points out.

We are near a splitting up. The train is slowing down. We stand about 30 feet apart. We must jump about the same time and take good stock of oncoming objects and measure the speed and the distance. If you are sure of yourself, then catch it immediately and hold on firmly. This train does not move as fast as the one in Toledo. We already had our experience there and we now feel quite capable to match ourselves with the other guys. There was no caboose attached to this train. "No caboose. It is no express, so we can jump on it easily," the leader shouts. The locomotive engineer glances at us in a careless way. He did not care about it and shammed donkey. He knew these hobos. Every year again it was the same game. The railroad police should see to that. It was not his business.

The huge wagons are close. We must jump now, because the others did so too. I manage to catch hold of a handle sticking out at the rear end of a tankwagon—first with my right hand, then, on the lower end of the handle, with my left hand. With my right foot I land on a ridge alongside, about a foot wide and sufficient to stand on firmly. I pull up my left foot and have it landed on the ridge too. I have to keep tight as the wagon sometimes shakes terribly.

The weather was cold. I had no idea how far we had to travel. I watched the other guys. When they would jump off I had to follow. Jörgen stood on a tank wagon, two wagons further. Looking back along the train I no longer saw anybody stand near the track, so the whole gang had made it. Once in awhile I saw a head sticking out. We rode for hours at a stretch, sometimes slow and then I could relieve one foot for the other, sometimes very fast and then I got very cold. We had to hold on firmly as the train began to shake like if there were an earthquake. We passed a train going in the opposite direction. It was a freight train twice as long as ours and I am sure I saw men hanging on it and sitting on top; a lot more men than we had on our train. It must have been tramps, for hobos like we just went out West to find work. Tramps do not work. It puzzled me how they kept alive. "The railroad dicks have a deep grudge upon them," our leader told us. "If they got to lay hands on them, they sure get some beating."

In our hotel he had told us before we went about the constellation of the American railroad system. The companies were all private concerns; there were more than twenty companies, perhaps many more. They all tried to make profits and therefore they used their rolling stock as long as possible. This is the reason why this latter was often in bad repair. "You guys will see by yourselves in what condition most of the wagons are in which you climb," he had said. I reflected on what he had told us and I closely examined with my eyes the wagons I could see. In my country, in Holland and also in Germany and France, the railroads were run by the government. The taxpayer, in fact, had to pay for their maintenance.

Near Marshalltown the train stopped for fresh water and fuel for the locomotive. We had to get off and hide somewhere because there were railroad dicks around. They did not catch sight of us. When the train started to move we again boarded it and took the same place we had before. We passed Ames. The leader had told us we should keep aloof now. "In these counties they are mad about hunting hobos, and certainly tramps," he said. We had decided that near Boone we should get off the train. This was the best place to start trying to get a job either as a hired man on a farm or as a corn picker.

To our amazement the train began to slow down a good many miles before Boone. We had not reckoned with this. We heard the piercing sound of a police whistle and then we saw three detectives armed with a gun running along the train, looking for unlawful train passengers. It was obviously meant for us. There was nothing else to it than to get off by our own free will and report at the police office. This was the best thing for us to do under the circumstances. And it might be the only way to try to avoid punishment. The railroad guard was housed not far from the station in a little wooden barrack, which had two rooms. We had to walk down there over the tracks. We were received by a couple of policemen, who searched us on weapons and asked for our papers, if at least we had these. None of us had papers. We must explain why we travelled on the train illegally.

"Where d'ye fellers come from and where'd you intend to go?" they asked us. Jörgen and I in turn were asked the same question and we truthfully told our story. While we did so, the door was opened and two other dicks entered, bringing in another offender. We thought it was a tramp. Anyway he did not belong to our company. We had not seen him before. The policemen had him grabbed at his shoulders, keeping his right arm high behind his back; he could not make any movement. It looked to us that he had offered resistance against the dicks. I heard them report to the men behind the table that the tramp had tried to get away after he got off the train and was summoned to stand still. It was a big blonde fellow, a "prizefighter" you might call him—a guy with a big mouth who I am sure would never be given any job by any farmer because of his impudence. He challenged the dicks who held him to fight them one at a time. "I'll beat the guts out'a you," he shouted. "Oh yeah?" one of the dicks said, "come on, baby, to the other room. We'll see you do it." They went into the other room and almost immediately we heard hoarse screams and dull groans followed by hard beatings. There seemed to be quite a commotion. It lasted a few minutes and then there was a silence. Very soon again the policemen came back into our room with the prizefighter, hanging face down, between them. His mouth was bleeding and one of his eyes swollen, while his jacket was torn up. "All right, baby, now say that again—come on, say it. Don't you dare to? Well, then we'll lock you in for a while," one of the dicks said. And he was taken away.

I was terrified. If this was the way they acted on tresspassing of the law, however trifling, I could not very well appreciate it. Neither did the others, to judge from the expression on their faces. Our leader told the policemen this guy did not belong to our little group and that we only tried to get work in the cornfields. Because we had no money, we had taken the liberty to jump on a freight train for just a little ride to get off somewhere about here. "All right, all right," the interrogator said, "you behaved all right. You may go on condition you won't touch any freight train as long as you are in our territory—and that is a big one! We'll play close attention to that. Should you be caught again, you can reckon on being punished severely." And on we went.

"You should never oppose those dicks and surely not the way this stupid tramp did," said our leader. "You'd give them the opportunity to give you a beating, and that's worse than the third degree. Well, you guys must forget about it." We proceeded our way to Boone, following the railroad tracks. In Boone, the club was to be divided into four groups. Two men should go up north, two down south, two out west, and two east.

We said goodbye and wished everybody good luck; then we parted. Splitting up the group this way was to prevent that too many of us should apply for a job at the same time and at the same place. It might lead to disappointments when it came to who'd got the job and who not. As a matter of fact, it would be a mere hit if we could find work at all right away.

Jörgen and I should go down south. Faint with hunger we bought a loaf of bread and an ounce of butter in Boone. We made short work of the eating and we ate it in no time. Satisfied, we turned our steps in the southern direction. This time we walked beside the tracks of the interurban, the railroad that catered for the transport of passengers and goods about the surrounding communities. As a venture we walked till we reached the little town of Kelley, where we stopped to try our luck. We had to, for we were practically broke. Our appearance needed some fashioning, so we headed for the barbership, the only one in town.

Barber Bill—I never found out what was his family name—

mustered us reflectively, puffing speckles of tobacco on the plank floor covered with streaks of human hair of all colors. Six men sat on wooden chairs, standing against the walls, waiting for their turn. There was a noise of voices, which ceased the moment we came in and got seated. We listened to the talk of the farmers who had broken up their conversation and were waiting for a shave or a haircut. I heard one of them—Dave, they called him—relating to the men about someone they knew well. "Jimmy, the son of Joe Young, bought a bran' new car, a Rickenbacker, a swell one. He made a ten-dollar bet with Dean Larsen he'd keep in pace with the Chicago North Western. He then raced along the road beside the railroad track the other day, the train moving with a speed of more'n 60 miles an hour. And Jimmy just kept up with it. So he won ten bucks. He sure's quite a guy."

"Ford's got a new sedan," a farmer said. "I know all about these Ford cars. They're the cheapest on the market. I just walk, that's the best for your body. I won't drive a stinking car," said Bill. "You guys know all about walking," he continued to us. "You came here by walking, didn't you?" "Yes, we walked along the track from Boone. We come from the old country," Jörgen answered. The men around pricked up their ears. "You hear that, fellahs, they're from the old country," said Bill, "I bet you're from Norway." "You guessed right," Jörgen said. "I'm Dutch," I said in my turn. Some guy in the corner shouted, "Why eh he'd come from where Carl Rosenfeld comes from, don't you?" he addressed me. "The name sounds German to me. I don't come from Germany. I'm from Holland, the Netherlands." "We haven't had a Dutchman around so far," said a man, who was called by the name of Morris. "Old Teddy Roosevelt's parents came from Holland." "I know," I said, "they were born in the province of Zeeland in the south of the Netherlands. The Dutch were the first to settle in New York, which they called New Amsterdam at the time," I said. "And Peter Stuyvesant, the Dutchman who had come from Holland in 1647, surrendered Manhattan later to the English. Afterwards the name was changed to New York. I was there. I worked there."

The farmers listened to me attentively. They were all ears to what those foreigners were telling them by heart. They seemed to be impressed. They themselves had learned it in school. They seemed to be amazed those guys knew so much about their history. "Anyway, you fellahs 're new around here," Bill said inquiringly between the noise, shifting his tobacco quid from one cheek to the other. "Looking for work, ain't you?" he sputtered. "Yes," I said, "we need it badly, we're almost broke." "You hear that, guys," he addressed the farmers who had continued their chat. "Clever boys, here. Anybody's willing to give 'em a job? Or knows about one?" he added. I strained my ears.

"Why, eh . . . yes. I guess I know a few who need help." The sound came from a corner near the door. "Clyde knows of someone, Clyde Finch," said Bill. "I believe I know a couple of farmers who can have you as hired men; but you must at least qualify. It's hard work. How about your experience? Have you guys done farm work?" he asked. "No, not the way its done here," I said. And Jörgen added, "We'd like to work hard." "Why . . . eh . . . that will do, I think," Clyde said.

We eagerly grasped the opportunity; it meant money. We were not afraid of hard work. We sure had some experience in Johnstown. I only hoped it would pay reasonably. "We'll take whatever job there is offered," I said. "We're about broke," added Jörgen, "we've just a couple of dollars left." Clyde Finch invited us to his farm to talk it over. He expected us about one in the afternoon so we could talk and see how to fix an arrangement.

After we had our shave we felt much relieved and so we went to Clyde's farm, situated to the south of Kelley. Clyde and his wife Mabel received us kindly and invited us for dinner. Mabel sized up the new arrivals and scanned us from top to toe. It was apparent she'd never seen such uncommon farm-hands before. The dinner was substantial and well done; we had not eaten so well for a long time.

After dinner we were set to work. We had to grind a little pile of corn in the grinding machine. Clyde showed us how to do it. It was meant for feeding the young cattle; the flour was to be mixed with skim milk, what made excellent grub for the heifers and the little pigs. Clyde went to see the farmers he had talked about and we started work.

When Clyde returned we had ground so much that he had enough feed for at least a week, which he did appreciate. He gave us the names and addresses of the farmers we could apply for work and who, he said, would sure take us because they had no hired help at present. Jörgen would go to Ole Cleveland

It is believed that all barbers in the Middle West are named "Bill." Should the nation's intelligence agencies be able to make use of Bill's knowledge of local affairs, they'd make a nice haul. For Bill knows all about everyone, and any event or occurrence sooner becomes known at the barbershop than when mentioned in the newspaper.

and I to Hans Ekeland, both farmers of Norwegian origin. Clyde had arranged that we would present ourselves that evening. We wondered what had become of the other guys of our gang. We went back to Kelley before going to our addresses to see how things were there.

Kelley, Iowa

November, 1923-March, 1926

THE TOWN of Kelley lies amidst cornfields, one could say, in the heart of the state of Iowa. The countryside under the clear blue sky has the atmosphere so typical of the Middle West. It differs from the other states. The vocal accent of the inhabitants and their idiom is easy to follow by foreigners like us. The land is flat and the views are extensive and Kelley, like all farm towns, has the characteristics of the area it belongs to. There is not much to see. At present—it is 1923—it is just a drab congregation of small buildings, divided by a street, Main Street. The town ends on its north side against the tracks of the interurban railroad. It consists, on one side of the street, of a local school, a few stores—a hardware store and a grocery, a barbershop, a bank, a drugstore—and a structure for cultural activities, a kind of a big barn, mostly used for the Saturday evening barn dancing. On the other side are a number of residences and an ice-cream bar, where you could drink a lemonade and eat an ice or a pie. Further along is a warehouse and a grain elevator, where the farmers deliver the corn they sold which is weighed and stored till it gets transported by rail. This elevator therefore is built near the tracks of the interurban—the railroad we walked along when we came from Boone. At the end of the street the tracks cross the street. Behind the crossing the road runs further to the south. In front of the grocery store at the edge of the sidewalk stand a couple of bars on four poles to which you can tie your horse when you come to town on horseback or by buggy. An occasional automobile completes the scenery of this quiet town. The busiest part of the street—if you may qualify this as busy—is near the barbershop, where people linger to have a chat.

At the moment we enter the town from the south, there all of a sudden is some bustling at the other end to the north. A

number of men approach from over the tracks, crossing them on the north side. They ride on horseback and each man leads one or more horses on the line. There is to be a horse swapping in town this afternoon. It generally is held in an open spot between the grocery and the drugstore and it brings quite a bunch of farmers to town. Horses were wanted anytime and a swapping gave the farmers of this neighborhood the opportunity to buy or change horses relatively cheap, and they could take them along right away.

84

The Midwest town of Kelley. A hired man in his free time directs his first steps to the nearest town, dull though it may be. And Kelley, Iowa, is a dull congregation of small premises. The biggest is the elevator where the corn is delivered. Wagons and horses form the "traffic" rather than do automobiles. Once in awhile you'll hear the noise of it and then everyone turns around to see who it is who's coming to town. The clerk of the bank, who is the boss himself, counts the dough deposited to the savings books, and the grocer pulls open a sack of potatoes at the entrance of his shop, while a riding horse, sleepily standing beside the sidewalk, eyes it all. Then, all of a sudden there's a turbulent noise—the interurban train booms by at the crossing at the end of the quiet Main Street. A cart fully loaded with husked corn enters town; the farmer sold his crop to the elevator.

We first went to the ice-cream shop to treat ourselves on a cone of ice cream. There were a number of people in the shop for the same reason. They stood at the counter enjoying their dainties. I heard a guy whisper to another, "What chaps are that?" A big fellow said, "They seem to be new around here." The big man then addressed me and asked, "Where you come from?" "We come from Pennsylvania," Jörgen said. "Lots of foreigners and aliens there," the big man said. And he continued, "Too many—we don't like to have them here to have our communities polluted with Negroes, Jews, and other nonwhites like in Pennsylvania." He said it in a conceited manner. "What has that to do with us?" I asked him. "You seem to be white, others are not. Ain't that enough?" "I am American born and we sure have to take care that America remains white. If you'd like to be adopted here, you'll have to behave like real Americans," the big man said, "otherwise you just as well hook it," he added kind of jokingly. "I don't like hired help; I rather do the work myself. No strangers around me." "Well," I said, "don't worry about us; we won't bother you. We're too white for you. Besides, it is none of your business how we'd like to behave." The other guy did not say much. He thought the conversation turn out to be kind of awkward. But the big man gave evidence that he was not quite fond of aliens—of people he could not identify with his own "breed," people who did not belong to his smart set of "real" Americans, as he put it.

It was the first time I was confronted with a man who had not the least notion of human dignity. I was disgusted and despised his way of thinking, if he thought at all. My disgust about his attitude was fortified when I remembered I had read in the newspapers about the racial outrages of the Ku Klux Klan, a secret society using the "fiery cross" as a warning to Negroes, Jews, Roman Catholics and to all those who did not fit in the thinking pattern of these "keeping-America-white" supermen. "Come on, Jerry," Jörgen said, "let'm lick his white ice." "Let's go to the horses," I said, "better get some horse sense. I don't like that big guy."

We had not the least experience with horses. I had hardly ever touched one in my life; it must have been that of the greengrocer when I was a little kid. Some of the farmers mustered us with a searching look. Our khaki clothes had their special attention. "These guys'd come from an army camp," I heard a man say to another. "Well," I said to him, "as soon as we've got earned some money, we'll dress the way you'd like us to. Will that do?" "All right boys," the farmer said, "you guys come from the old country?" And a little later he continued, "You know about horses?" We did not say much. Jörgen looked at a little horse that shyly tripped when pulled at its rope. "You like to ride 'em?" the owner said to Jörgen. "Yes, why not?" he replied. The man released the horse. Jörgen took a run and jumped on its back from behind. Almost immediately the horse bolted away, taking him along on its back. First it kicked with its hind legs in the air. Then it took a run like a fast train. I saw Jörgen cling to the horse's mane with efforts. He jumped up and down, which sure must have been painful to him, for he had no saddle. The farmer, who had invited him to ride his horse, looked a little confused. He, in fact, could see Jörgen wasn't used to horses at all. He seemed to be afraid the horse might throw him off and he felt himself responsible for that greenhorn. It lasted more than half an hour before Jörgen turned up. He still sat on horseback, triumphantly waving one of his arms. The horse meekly trotted near. The farmers looked surprised. Perhaps those newcomers weren't such duffers after all. We had made it; we were accepted.

Afterwards Jörgen told me he had kneeled his knees against the flanks of the horse because he had no reins. The horse just could not buck. It was quite easy for him. It spread like wildfire that the two newcomers were going to be the hired men of Ole Cleveland and Hans Ekeland. The biggest of the two, the one who was to go to Ole Cleveland, had ridden a "bronco" and "broke" it. This rumor, naturally, was a practical joke, for the farmers who swapped horses darned well knew about how bucking broncos were to be broken actually. Jörgen's horse had been broken long before he got on his back; it'd only gotten nervous.

In the evening I presented myself to Hans Ekeland. Hans was a hard-working farmer, a kind of a humorless man. His wife, an amiable quiet woman, seemed to be pleased with my appearance. They had a son, two years old, and there was a grandma living with them. The latter represented the "gamle Norge"; her grandson was a "store gutt"—she only spoke Norwegian. Hans Ekeland was willing to pay me forty dollars a month with board and lodging, which I accepted.

Hans' face wore the signs of the seasons of Iowa—in summer, hot, in winter, severely cold. Farmers have that expression, working outdoors most of their life. I thought it must be a monotonous life, riding behind the horses' hinds all day long, plowing, edging, spreading manure, harvesting, and so on. His land was rich, the soil excellently suited for big corn crops.

The Middle West is an immense area, fertile with good black earth on which corn, wheat, and oats thrive abundantly and of grassy pastures on which you see occasional herds of cattle. In winter it was a vast white blanket. Hans already very soon entrusted to me part of the winter plowing to do all alone by myself. I was just a small-sized guy, not acquainted with farm work, but I nevertheless did the heavy work the way it ought to be done. And so I worked that first winter on the Iowan farm. It was long, hard, and dirty work and I could imagine that many of the younger farm-bred people gradually were seeking a gentler way of living in the towns or in more southerly and westerly areas of the U.S.A., far from the Cornbelt.

When the winter had passed and soft weather heralded spring, Hans charged me with the spring plowing with the two-bottom plow. This big plow was drawn by seven horses, three in front and four in the back. It sure was heavy work for an inexperienced man like me. I had to drive seven horses and to hold four reins. The furrows should be plowed in straight lines and this could only be done by holding the horses steady. Turning for the next furrow was another problem. After turning my double team and making them pull the plow close to the furrow that had been done, I had to throw the plowshares into the ground at the right moment, getting up the horses to have them pull at the same time. I was amazed of myself that I could manage it. I must confess, though, that I had a bunch of excellent horses at my disposal.

If I made a wrong move, it was rectified by Belle, my best horse, who just kept on walking to the right furrow; she apparently knew more about the art of plowing than I. But all the same, horses were horses and whatever they achieved and however obedient they were, they remained nervous animals. You had to handle them with care. Once I nearly had a runaway when I was hitching up four horses to the harrow. One of the horses got scared by some sound I did not hear and jerked at the lines. The others, too, got scared and nervously pulled up to the other side. At that moment I pulled the wrong rein and in no time the horses got entangled in their harnesses. I could not get them out of the tangle and shouted to Hans, who luckily came in time to calm them down and allay a panic. It was good luck the horses had not stepped on the iron harrow; they might have wounded their legs. Had I been alone to myself, I should not have known how to get them out of the knot. And I sure had learned a lesson as to the horses' behavior.

The horses had a fine stable. This was Hans's pride. His horses and livestock were the first to be cared for and they should have the best lodging, more than he himself and his family and the hired man. His house was simply accommodated, with only the most necessary furniture. His barns, stables, and sheds, however, were provided with all implements that may give animals the comfort they needed to grow fat and to have a good rest. Human beings could take care of themselves; livestock and horses could not and should therefore be spared.

He also took great care of his machines and tools. We folks were considered to be of secondary importance and only needed a table to eat on, chairs to sit on, and a bed to sleep in—and sleep well—for the beds were excellent.

His barns were built on quite a distance from the house, which was very progressive. Many farmers had their house nearby the farm buildings. It did not matter much, because most of the time they remained in the field, the barn, the sheds, or the stables. They only came into the house to eat and sleep.

Hans possessed 280 acres of fertile farmland. The corn crop we harvested when I worked for him in the late fall yielded a great number of bushels per acre, thanks to his expert farming. He was in a way a progressive farmer, seemingly, because he owned a Chevrolet automobile, an open sedan, green colored. He therefore was in my eyes a big farmer. On warm days the soft top of the car could be let down. Most of the time, though, he rode his buggy when he went to Kelley. These buggies all had the same model throughout the country. They consisted of a short little carriage on four high, tiny wheels and they had a linen cover that could be let down or set up according to the weather conditions. It was drawn by one horse. These buggies were snug little cars and I sure liked to ride in them.

Like all farmers of the Middle West, Hans was a kind of egocentric man. His democracy resided in his surroundings and in what happened within his intimate sphere of interest. What happened outside and had nothing to do with farming fell beyond his point of view. He could not allow anything to interfere with his way of living or to harm his property, even the smallest. His harshness in this respect became evident to me one day when a nomadic cat had killed a number of his chickens. He kept on the lookout, having laid a bait. He was convinced the monster'd come back sometime. He finally got hold of it and he killed it right away, catching it by the tail and

*Not every farmer possesses an auto-
mobile because he does not see the use
of it and maybe he does not have the
money yet to buy one. Why shouldn't a
buggy be just as cosy? Horses are always there and their fuel is raised by
the farmer himself. They won't be up
against want of gasoline like the automobiles. And in most cases also the
postman delivers the mail at the farmhouse by buggy and puts his stuff into
the P.O. box.*

---

beating its head with tremendous force against the wall. The
cat fought for its life with all that was in it and it shrieked
horribly. But it was of no use; after five hard blows it was done
with it.

The working days began at five in the morning. The first I
had to do was milking the cows in the stable. Contrary to the
beef cattle, the milk cows were inside in midwinter. They could
not stand the severe cold. The beef cattle were used to it; they
could stand colds of more than twenty degrees below zero and
they stayed outside all winter. But Hans had not such cattle; he
only kept to dairying, milking about twenty cows. When
milking was done, we had breakfast. I stayed with Hans until
October 1924. Then Cap Accola asked me to come to his place
and work for him. My pay would be fifty dollars a month with
board and room up in the house.

I reacted positively on his offer and a month later I moved
to Rural Route 3, where Cap's farm was situated. He owned
380 acres of fertile land. Three hundred acres were intended
for corn and oats, the other acres for hay—mostly alfalfa or
clover—and for pasture. Cap had a herd of fine small Jersey
cows, which gave rich milk with the highest percentage of

cream. This latter was separated by a centrifuge called a separator.

On the whole the work I had to do and the number of working hours were the same as with Hans Ekeland. The breakfast, however, was more tasty, for Suzy, the mistress, baked the most delicious hotcakes, a kind of flapjack, that were eaten with warmed honey. I digested a respectable pile of them in the early morning after I had been milking with the milking machine, stripping them afterwards. This milking-machine consisted of an electric motor, driving—by means of a belt—a long rod, fastened along the barn in front of the cows, moving it to and fro. On this rod a number of pumps were rigged that alternatively sucked the air from the hoses and the four mouthpieces attached to the udders. In this way six cows could be milked at the same time. At seven, the horses were harnessed for plowing or other work. The heaviest work was haying and threshing. Threshing oats took a lot of preparations prior to setting the threshing machine to work and having the oats separated. Cap had a tractor—a Twin City—that furnished the power, using a long drive belt (about 50 feet long); it had one twist in the middle. In this part of the Midwest the gasoline motor for the use of threshing was in vogue for quite a long time already, although in some parts of Iowa they still used the steam thresher. But these became more and more obsolete. The long belts with a twist, however, remained indispensable also with the gasoline engine.

The shocks of oats had to be thrown into the machine and I had to haul them. Another man was put in the straw stack to level the straw as it came blown out of the machine. It was a dirty job. Sometimes the straw was thrown into the barn and this was a still dirtier job. It all was a lot of work, but in the end of the run, about eleven, we usually had a get-together with an ice-cream social, which sure was a breath spell.

For the mistress in particular threshing time was a nervous time, especially when the day came the thresher was made ready to get used. Then all neighbors from around came over to assist. In most cases the thresher with the crew was rented for that day. It went from one farm to another. Cap was one of the few who owned a threshing outfit himself, together with the Wilsons and the Roneys, who were neighbors. Apart from the outfit itself, some seven or eight teams of horse wagons—the one of ourselves and those of the neighbors— came to haul the oats shocks from the field and throw them into the machine. Disregarding the mostly hot weather, everyone did his best to get the crop in. At half time, late noon, all farmers and farmhands came from the field to have a good lunch; they were all seated around big tables. When the weather was good, the lunch was eaten in the open in the farmyard; otherwise, it had to be done inside and then it was kind of crowded. At the table quite a good yarn was spun. And in this way threshing time was enacted, one by one, from farm to farm in turn. The young farmer-sons and the hired men then had a good time and ample opportunity to get in touch with the farmers daughters; one never could tell.

Cap had his tractor for a variety of heavy duties. There were not so many tractors in use at that time. But the tendency prevailed to substitute horse and man power by mechanical power. In the twenties, though, a good farmhand was still in demand. Haying was done end of June, beginning of July. With the mower, having five-foot scissors, the hay was cut and then had to be dried about twenty-four hours. It then got raked to long rows of heaps by the raking machine and after it had dried a little more it was raked again. After three days, with the hope of dry weather, the hay was ready to be taken in. With the pitchfork it was loaded high on the carts and driven to the barn. Most of the time it was hot weather during this operation and we drank a lot. Also, the ice-cold watermelons we fished out of the water basin at the pump mill were a delicious treat.

When all summer work was finished we had more spare time. In this time of the year somewhere to the north of Des Moines the Iowa State Fair was held and we sure went up there on some leisure day.

Winter made its entry and the time was there again to get the corn crop in. Picking corn was mostly done in November and early December, when the frost had gone over the stalks. I already knew much about the methods of cornhusking. The year before, after the freight train ride, I had done some husking at Hans's farm and I saw corn pickers everywhere in the fields. In the early winter all stalks and leaves were withered and yellow. In this condition you could easily grasp the ears at sight and hurl them against the high catch board on the wagon. Cornhusking by hand was an art in itself. In the big cornfields of Cap I soon got more practice in trying to pick corn like the old diehards did—tear away the leaves with the pick hook and tear off the corn ear.

While I was busy picking corn I reviewed in my thoughts the times before my going to sea. As a boy I often roamed about the quays of our big port of Rotterdam, the town where I was born, and looked at the floating elevators sucking out of the sea ships the grain that was to be transshipped—grain that had come from America and Canada. The big silos stood near the Rijnhaven and the Maashaven loaded to the roof so as to enable the factories to work up the grain. And then to know that I now was helping to harvest this grain. What happened to it afterwards I could easily understand; the whole world should be eating it, the farmers earned on it, and so did the railroads, the big shipping lines, and the bakers.

Quite soon I husked like an old hand. I could not think of ever taking part in the cornhusking contests that were held every year. It would take years to become an experienced husker. When we rode the freight train and got off at Boone, the corn pickers among the gang told us that the wage rate for husking corn generally was about five cents per bushel. If you worked hard and made long hours you could husk from 80 to 100 bushel a day. The techniques of husking by hand were like this. You had a leather strap fastened to your right hand, with a steel hook, on the inner side, about in the middle of the palm of the hand. With your left hand you tore aside the corn ear and with the hook you ripped off the leaves on the right side of the ear. Almost immediately you took with your left hand the leaves on the other side away and with your right hand you jerked the ear fastly off the shank. With a uniform motion you hurled the ear in the direction of the bangboard on the wagon, which kept in pace with you. Now that I was actually engaged in the farm business, I tried to put the wise lessons of the guy into practice. I soon got the taste of picking corn and in order to resist the monotony of the tiresome job I made it a game to hurl the ears with the utmost force and with regular intervals against the wooden bangboard that was fixed on top of the wagon. In this way I obtained a certain cadence, the rhythm of which set me to speed up husking. If I did not hear a bounce, I had missed the board. I then had to take it more easy. I finally obtained a frequency that kept me in pace with the horses that pulled the wagon. I noticed that my routine grew gradually. The horses pulled up step by step—they were very obedient to my "get-ups" and "whoas."

"Whoa!" "Giddap!" "Bang!"
There goes the ear against
the high bangboard. Husking
corn by hand with the pick
hook—a weary job. But then
when the wagon is full, you
have your satisfaction.

Part of the corn crop was transported to the elevator in Kelley belonging to a company that bought the corn from the farmers, shelled it, and sold it afterwards when the market was favorable. Ole Brendeland was in charge, a skinny man with a red mustache. He was a hard worker who was always willing to help you fix the wagon. When the wagon was on the weigh bridge it was pivotted backwards so the corn could slide out onto the transport belt moving the load into the silo.

Another part of the corn crop was stored by the farmers in their own corncribs. For this purpose Hans Ekeland had a transport system, moved by horses which walked around with a big pole that turned a kind of a merry-go-round fastened to the belt. Through a hatchway high up in the wall of the crib the corn was deposited into the inside. Cap, too, had an elevator belt like Hans's; it was, however, moved by his tractor. This elevator also made it possible to blow the fodder to the top of the silo, loading it full up. In this way part of the crop was silaged to be used for cattle feed during the winter. Before

going into the silo the corn was cut by a binder, which tied the fodder into bundles. The bundles were then loaded on flat wagons, hauled to the cutter, and from there, blown into the silo. The cutter too was driven by the tractor by means of a long belt with one twist. The cutter machine had sharp knives attached to a paddle wheel; they cut the fodder in little pieces about half an inch, after which it was blown with great force over the top into the silo. When the corn was in, we could take it a little easier and we had more time for ourselves.

I had bought me a horse to enable me to get to town easily and to visit my friends whenever I'd like to. It was allowed to partake in the feeding of Cap's animals. It was an obedient, quiet horse that had a good gait. I called her "Speedy." On Saturdays everyone speeded up work because you'd got more time left to go to Kelley or Ames. Generally the family had its own affairs. So had I, and when the chores were done and we had eaten, I jumped on horseback and galloped as fast as I could to Barber Bill to have myself fixed up. As I earned a good wage I was in the position to save some money and I could afford to buy me the style of dress I liked. When I arrived in Kelley I lined my horse to the fence on the curb before the grocery store. Often, however, I left Speedy home and went to town lifting with someone going that way. In the night or on the following morning, when I went home, some guy often took me along with his car.

It was spring 1925. We started plowing. Cap took his tractor with the two-bottom plow and I took the horses and plowed with the single plow. Edging was done solely with the horses. The farmers community around Kelley and Ames consisted of people having roots in the European countries. So Morris Noring descended from the British, Clyde Finch from the Irish, Cap Accola from the Swiss, Ole Cleveland and Hans Ekeland from the Norwegians, Carl Rosenfeld from the Germans, and perhaps there were more descendants from other nationalities. I was Dutch and although I was not naturalized I was taken up in this community of multinationals. There probably had been reasons for the settlement of so many progressive farmers, namely, the neighboring Iowa State College. These instances where they could get as much advice as possible on farming problems were close at hand.

Cap and his wife Suzy—who was a Gfeller daughter, Sue we called her—were nice people. Cap was a medium-sized man. He walked somewhat face down and he dragged a little with his left leg. He often wore his square cap with flaps on both sides, which were let down in winter to prevent frozen ears. In his mouth he invariably pinched his corncob pipe. If he got mad at me for doing something wrong, he called me "shyster," an expression that probably was derived from his Swiss descent. Long ago Cap had his left hand pinned between some machinery; he never talked about it. He could not use it to its full strength. I wondered that he could play his clarinet so well when using his mutilated hand. And he sure was a crack in playing this instrument. Cap had black hair and clear blue eyes. Had these outward signs been endowed to a woman, she'd been called a beauty. The Accolas were of a hard-working kind and Cap expected the full 100 percent of his hired man. I believed he needed not have any doubt about that with respect to me. I was active all day long and I tackled my job in such a way that I even found time to relax.

Contrary to most old farmhouses, Caps' house was warmed in winter from the basement to the attic. In the basement stood a big "Advance Windsor" stove that had enough capacity to warm the whole house. In every room there was a grating in the ceiling that could be opened and closed. In winter it was kept open so the warmth could stream upwards. My room was the highest—on the third floor—and caught the least of the warmth. I therefore jumped into my bed as fast as I could to prevent that I lost the little bit of the warmth I had. Once a week I took a bath in the bathtub that stood in the attic. In winter it was really cold in my sleeping room, even though it was warmed through the opening in the floor. The attic was often below zero, but all the same I took my bath. Taking a bath in summer was quite simpler. Most of the time I just jumped into the basin of the windmill outside, or I took a couple of pails of water to the barn.

Very soon I was taken up in the family. I thought maybe my background, too, had accounted for this. I had told them about my work as a wireless operator on board ships and about the study that had preceded it. And I behaved myself like if I really was a member of the family. On Sunday mornings I went to church with them, neatly dressed, my shoes polished. Attentively I listened to the sermon and I sure believed the service did some good to my soul. When the community sang the psalms I firmly joined for I loved to sing. After church we either stayed home or went out for a visit.

From my earnings I had bought a mandolin because I

meant I should take part in the musical activities of the Accola family. Cap himself played the clarinet and I believed he played in a chamber orchestra and also in church performances. The eldest son, Lowell, played the trombone, and he often played in some band performances. Glen, the youngest of the two boys, was too young to add to the musical aspects and he rather liked galloping through the fields on the back of his Shetland pony. I must confess I did not know a note of music. All the same, however, I managed to play most of the top tunes of the gay twenties by heart—hits like "All Alone," "Follow the Swallow Back Home," "Pretty Little Blue-eyed Sally," and last, but not least, I excelled in playing the Iowa Corn Song, "I'm from Iowa, that's where the tall corn grows."

There was not much time left for making music. The Saturday and Sunday were the only days I was free to do what I liked. I divided my free time between shopping, going to church with the family, and spending the weekends with newly made friends like Ole Cleveland and Lars Thorsten who had a pretty daughter. I had not seen Jörgen for quite awhile. He soon had left Ole Cleveland to start to work for Lars. He had told me about his intentions at the time and I suspected what were his motives to change the big farm of Ole for that of the crofter Lars. Well, I guessed his sexual ambitions needed a new relationship. Brit Thorsten was a lovely girl. He probably was out to gradually lead up to go courting her. In my secret heart I

The chores done—no more manure pitching, milking, finishing, . . . and then dinner. Not much later you rush to Kelley and having had yourself fixed up by Barber Bill, you go up to the barn dance with a couple of friends, seeing the girls later. Or, you take your honey with you right away. Girls making themselves up—a lot of poudre de rouge and lipstick. After some talks and drinks you join in the square dance. The fiddlers keep on and on playing their tunes and the dance master calls his instructions as to the figures.

hoped he wouldn't get a chance. I did not like his ways of late. I never had really gotten familiar with him—I did not know why. Maybe I thought him kind of amoral.

On Saturdays I often stayed overnight with the Clevelands. That is to say, when Cap consented to my staying away and if the chores could be done by others. Lots of times I went to the barn dance in Kelley with Bertha Cleveland. Bertha was a good dancer and she taught me to dance the square dances and other country dances. I never before had partaken in country dances. In my native country, living in the big port of Rotterdam too far from the provinces where they practiced folk dancing, I never got the opportunity to join a party. So it was great fun to me to join the people in Kelley dancing the square dances. Once in awhile these country dances were diversified by the common classical dancing, like the waltz, the fox-trot, and the one-step.

Ole was not married. He ran his farm together with his Uncle Paul, who acted as a kind of a father to both Ole and Bertha; the latter in turn had the role of the mother. Their parents had died when they were young. They owned a big cattle farm. Ole was a cattle raiser and mainly bred feed cattle for the stockyards. He had always a big herd of heifers for this purpose. He betted on the market prices and speculated on the bears and bulls of the livestock market. He exactly followed the fluctuations of the prices in the newspapers and when these were favorable he would sell part of his herd, mostly short-horns, which were good beefcattle, and also some of his fattened heifers to the Union Stockyards in Chicago. As a matter of fact, Ole was rather more a speculator than a farmer, although he milked some cows and raised corn for feeding.

Most of all I longed for the Saturday evenings when the family took part in the community party that was held every fortnight at one of neighboring farm homes. We had a lot of fun, did games, and made music. And I sure would not miss the night at Duvall's home. Joe Duvall had three children—a boy Edwin and two girls, Dorothy and Gladys. Dorothy, the elder daughter, was a pretty and handsome girl. I had once gone with her to the movies in Des Moines and had fallen in love with her. Her dad, however, did not quite approve to it and held me at bay. In a way I could follow his motives, for I still was an alien. Besides, I had no farm background. Joe liked me, but he did not encourage me. Lucky for me I had other ambitions and was not very easily brought in the dumps. So, in fact, my life went on undisturbed.

My horse was dead. I found her one morning in the field, lying backwards in a narrow ditch, choked to death. She must have slid and fallen down into the ditch upside-down, her legs up in the air. She could no longer expand her sides and suffocated. I was sad about it for she was a nice and obedient horse. Without a horse I could not move the way I was used to. On a horse swapping in Kelley I bought me another horse. It was not a bronco but it sure was a fast horse, wiry and tawny. It trotted exemplary and when galloping it resembled a fast train. It was an excellent single footer, so I could sit on her back for hours at a stretch without getting tired. I called her "Bullet." She once threw me off. That occurred the first time I had to cover a longer distance. Riding somewhere along a country road I saw a number of cows dallying in a pasture; some of them were bully. Seeing this herd seemed to actuate something in her subconscience and all of a sudden, while I was not in the least prepared for it, she turned with a hook of ninety degrees and got after the cows, throwing me off. I rose from the ground and yelled to her to come back, adding some pithy expressions to it, and she came back, the ears back down. I believed she jolly well knew she went beyond her brief. Anyway, it looked that way, for she approached me very shyly. It never happened again. As soon as I observed cattle and felt her jerking her head in that peculiar way, I held the reins. It was a good horse that answered to the bridle and to my way of riding and she was almost indefatigable.

Once I had to go to Cap's brother Alfred at Alleman to fetch a young horse, a two-year old that had not been broken yet. Cap had bought her from his brother to replace a horse that had grown too old. I had to ride ten miles to Alfred's farm. Having had good hot coffee, I started to go back. I mounted "Bullet" to ride the ten miles back, in my right hand, the reins, in my left, the line tied to the halter of the young horse. It was cold and the frost tickled my face. I wore my thick sheepskin-lined macintosh and had on my feet my jackboots also lined with sheepskin. The first half mile the young animal meekly trotted beside me and "Bullet." At least I thought she was meek. But I had underestimated her. A few minutes later, she showed quite another attitude. She stopped and reared on her hind legs. She turned around, pulling my horse and me aside and started to run back to where she came from. I had no choice. I could not hold her and she tugged me back to Alfred's stable. We had to arrange another method and so we tied a rope around her upper lip with a gliding knot. As soon as she tried to have it her way I had to pull at the rope, which caused the knot to squeeze her nose. I went on my way again and she meekly trotted along all the way. She did not get a chance to buck and her sides foamed with sweat. I surmised, however, that she was not as docile as she looked like in her humiliating condition. Anyway, the nose rope compelled her to obey, though she remained an ornery horse. When I got back home after having ridden more than twenty miles to and fro, the young horse, tired to death and wet all over, was hitched to the fully loaded manure spreader. She had to pull the heavy cart over the field and when this was finished she was meek as a lamb and had herself led quietly to the stable—she sure was broken. The first time she remained kind of nervous and jumpy. One day I got to do with this. It happened I came behind her in the stable forgetting to say a few words, so she got scared and all at once kicked me on my bottom, one of her hoofs flatly beating my right hind end. As this was fleshy enough to absorb the blow nothing seriously happened.

I fully enjoyed riding on horseback and I could imagine how the cowboys of Wyoming and South Dakota felt in their element when riding their horses all day long. The cowboy generation had become practically extinct by this time, although the farmers still needed and rode horses to plow and to drive cattle to and from the pastures or to the railroad depots. Still, it was only about some twenty years ago that a number of notorious cattle thieves and bank robbers had galloped about the western states to get away from the threatening handcuffs of the sheriff. At that time of the cowboys and the buffalo hunters, Dodge City still was the cow capital of the West, although a lot of cattle already went to Chicago.

The milk rider of Story County, old Bill McLean, could tell a whole lot about them when he was in the mood. He had witnessed those horse devils when they were riding the "outlaw trail," as they called it. This trail ran from Montana along the Canadian border, crossed the Missouri River, and ran further via various hiding places in Wyoming, partly through Utah, Colorado, and Arizona, and when they might get cornered, finally to New Mexico. The trail was speckled with the hiding places of these gunmen, places no one knew about. Bill now was seventy years old. He transported the milk of the farmers to the creameries. He did not come to Cap's farm, because Cap skimmed the milk himself with the separator and took the cream to the factory himself. Originally Bill came from South

Dakota, where he was born, and in his youth he had learned to ride broncos. He had taken part in selling these to the farmers as the well-known Dakota horses. These were tough riding horses and very much in demand by the cowhands of that time. If Bill was not drunk, which was seldom the case, he might be in the mood to give a detailed account of what he had witnessed in his youth and what he himself had experienced in those roaring times in the western states when cattle thieves and robbers sought safety in the flight along the outlaw's trail. He told the following tale:

From Casper in eastern Wyoming they once in awhile took the Oregon trail into Nebraska, where they robbed a bank or some big store and they mostly vanished as fast as they had come, up north through South Dakota. They were unfindable and their chasers often were at a loss to figure out where they'd gone. They avoided Fort Laramie near the Nebraskan border and headed up north to the Deadwood stage route. This was in South Dakota, very near to where I was born. There were no hiding places good enough for them in South Dakota, so they just took some fresh horses from some farm and galloped back to their own trail via Sundance and Gillette, where they crossed the Powder River heading for the Great Wall and vanished through the "Hole in the Wall."

In spite of the fact that they were criminals, they were said to get admired by both the farmers and the sheriffs because of their daring exploits. As to Bill, he thought them just common criminals, without any romantic halo.

And Bill related:

The most notorious sure were Buck Cassidy (Rob Leroy Parker), Ben Kilpatrick (the Tall Texan), Kid Curry (the Tramp), Sundance Kid, and Georgie Parrott, with his big nose. The Sundance Kid came from Wyoming; he was born and raised in Sundance, a village near the frontier of South Dakota. All the same, they were cunning devils and they mostly formed a gang of five to ten men who had their own hiding places in the states of Montana, Wyoming, Colorado, and New Mexico. They always had fresh horses ready in these places to get away super fastly. Their dexterousness in disappearing baffled their chasers and no sheriff was capable to find the true evidence to indict them of a cattle or bank robbery. They even could walk the street as if they were as innocent as an angel because, as they stated, "We could never have had these crimes committed as it would have taken too much time for us to get away and be back already again.

"At last, however," Bill said,

the outlaw trail became known to justice and one by one the wild bunch was caught. Some of them were caught by surprise in the saloon they always came for a drink in Thermopolis. Kid Curry was notorious for his unnecessary killings and Big Nose George Parrott, who sometimes joined the gang of Butch Cassidy, also was a mean guy—he murdered like hell and shot everyone he did not like. When he was caught, the mob took him from jail and lynched him. One of the last who was executed was Black Jack Detchum; he was hung in New Mexico on the charge of train robbery.

Bill himself looked like the old cowboys. He wore the old cow hat and sat on the driving box calling loudly his giddaps

The greater part of Iowa farming de-
pends upon horses; they are indispens-
able. Hence the horse swappings held
every now and then in town. He who
wants to get rid of a horse can sell it
and farmers often exchange horses. An
ornery horse that all the same is a
good draft horse often is exchanged for
a bungling goody-goody because the
buyer thinks himself able enough to
handle the first. As a rule, he has to
pay in addition. There are traders who
do nothing else than run down farmers'
communities to barter their horses.
These ain't mustangs and broncos, for
these hardly exist anymore in the
Iowan regions—perhaps in Texas or
New Mexico. No, they mostly trade in
colts, mares, and geldings, and some-
times they swap a filly for a male foal.
Once in awhile you may see them sell
a mule, the unreliable but sturdy work-
er. Stallions, however, you will never
see at swappings. Those are bred by
farmers themselves and they are cod-
dled, for they are the sires of their
beautiful foals.

---

and whoas to his horse. I once witnessed he was sitting on the box early in the morning, drunken of the booze he had been drinking that night, and got a mad fit. He had drawn his old Colt and emptied it in the air. The firing aroused the people of Kelley, who said, "There's Bill McLean, he's got the staggers again." But then, it was only twenty years ago that the rawhides lived not so far from Iowa. Some of the horses that were swapped were of a breed caught by the old cowhands, their ancestors having been ridden by real cowboys. I once asked Bill, who had been driving his milk car for only ten years yet, whether he himself had taken part in these outlaw practices, but he said, "I never was that way. I just liked to live my life seriously and to run cattle."

Well, in the Dakotas the outlaws had not much chance to hide because the country was not suited for many hiding places. And in quiet Iowa there even was no place to drive a herd of cattle along the roads and there never were any cowboys.

There were not many hired men who had their own horse to ride like I did. In Kelley, in front of the grocery store, there stood a wooden crossbeam to which you could tie your horse. Jörgen also rode a horse once in awhile, which he lent from Lars Thorsten. I never could understand why he had left the big farm of Ole Cleveland for a small farm like the one of Lars. It was well known that he would never get a chance to have a love affair with Lars's daughter, Brit. At the Cleveland farm he could earn a lot more money.

Ole Cleveland, as I said already, was a cattle feeder. When his cattle had enough weight, he sold them. I did not know exactly where he bought his heifers. I thought somewhere in Nebraska, from where they were transported by rail to Kelley. The wagons were put on a sidetrack, from where the heifers were taken to the farm by motor truck or horse cart via the road. There was no use for cowboys here. The fatted cattle mostly was sold directly to Swift and Hammond, the big Chicagoan meat packers.

I not always stepped out on Saturday or Sunday. I also stayed home now and then, when it was my turn to do the chores and certainly when all the folks had to go somewhere. I then felt kind of lonesome and often confined myself to read a book or to make some music on my mandolin. I also passed the time with reading the extensive and voluminous newspapers, the *Des Moines Register* and the *Chicago Tribune.* I learned much of the American language by reading the funny papers, the features, and the comic strips like: "Barney Google" (with his goo-goo-googly eyes!) and "the Toonerville trolley that meets all the trains." It was great fun to me to understand the draw of a comic. I also sometimes read the *New York Times,* the circulation of which was distributed as far as the Great Lakes in the North and Florida in the South. The *Chicago Tribune* covered an area with a radius from Chicago halfway to Colorado. In the local press much attention is given to society news and I always went through these columns. Emphatically the offspring of the VIP who was interviewed was relevant as was the old country involved in the news. I, indeed, was fond of the news of what was happening in the U.S.A. and I read all that was published. I had followed the Sacco and Vanzetti case, of which I had the feeling it was more a question of the judge's trying to save their face—the judiciary against a bunch of radicals, and the public opinion, which is not always unprejudiced, against a certain political tendency (called Marxism). On account of these judicial squabbles, the two men were awaiting judgment for years already. I also read, among others, about the horrible murder on Bobby Franks, committed by Loeb and Leopold, two very intelligent 18-years old students, sons of rich parents. An ice-cold murder, committed only to see how a human being behaved when he died. They first tortured Bobby till he was dead. Thereupon they hurled the body in a lime pit to wipe out all evidence. But they forgot one thing—a small piece of the glasses of Bobby Franks that had broken off. This put the police on the track of the criminals. This atrocious murder aroused a wave of horror among the people of the U.S.A. and public opinion demanded the death penalty for the sadists. The famous crime lawyer, Clarence Darrow, attained the conversion of the death penalty to a life sentence, to which the wealthy state of the parents might have contributed. In this way I spent my Sunday afternoons in loneliness.

One Sunday I happened again to be alone. All was quiet and no sound was to be heard. Still, there was something that called my attention, though I could not say what it was. The door giving entrance to the back kitchen stood ajar and I rose to close it. I felt kind of uneasy; I could not say why. Although I only heard the stillness, I must have felt there was something behind that door and so I just opened it again to look behind it. And then I got the scare of my life. There stood a guy staring at me with discomfort. It was a tramp, to judge from his appearance. He must not have washed for weeks, perhaps for months, and he had a dirty stubble beard. He did not say a word and just stood there eyeing me inquiringly. I reacted immediately and got devilish at the stinker. "Why don't you knock with your dirty paws instead of sneaking behind the door and leering inside? What the hell you're up at. I've a mood to punch your nose." The man shrunk and made a move to turn and get away. "I'd like to have something to eat," he muttered. "Oh," I said, "if you're hungry, just say so, then I get you some. Now, come on in and keep your dirty hands off things. You should have a wash once in awhile. I'll get you something to eat."

This tramp had strayed quite a distance from the railroad

tracks. Their way of travelling again and again was jumping freight trains. They never worked and just moved and begged or stole. They were good-for-nothing bastards. Suzy hated those riff raffs, the more so as they always stood sneaking behind doors. She'd rather have me hunt 'em away and Cap, too, said he'd never allowed them to get into the kitchen.

I could not bring myself to send him away without giving him something to eat. I had found it to my cost myself and I knew how it felt to be hungry. Maybe it would have been better to chase him away because those tramps had the usage to leave some sign for their confederates to tell them that in this house they had a chance to get some grub. Well, I'd keep an eye on that. I gave him bread and cheese and poured him a cup of coffee. When he left he grumbled a few words of thank and disappeared.

The time of the high school final exams was over and everywhere there were festivities in the homes and also in the schools. Cap was chairman of the school council of the Napier Consolidated Schools and therefore had a voice in the chapter. We all had to attend the school festive evening at the Kelley High School. Lowell ordained me to take my mandolin with me, for he had fixed up that I, too, had to play a tune. It was not quite my intention to do so, but I would not disappoint him, and so I took it with me. And, as I had expected, after awhile there was a cry from some corner in the hall and I heard the boys and girls yelling, "Jerry must play, Jerry must play." I did not get a chance to back out and so I had to go to the platform with my mandolin. I felt very small, but nevertheless started to twang my instrument and I played a number of tunes, well known to the youthful audience. I played "Bye, bye, Blackbird," "Follow the Swallow Back Home," "Pretty Little Blue-eyed Sally" and I closed with "the Iowa Corn Song," the whole audience joined in singing and when I hit a wrong note they just shouted my music down. There was a wild screaming in the far end of the hall, near to where Lowell and his friends were seated. My suspicions went in his direction and my intuition told me their fun had something to do with my playing. They cheered me too vociferously and I surmised it was more a question of making fun than of showing esteem for my musical interpretation. The moment they joined in singing to accompany my tunes, it sounded more like a musical treat.

Anyway, they showed a lot of enthusiasm for the hired man's performance. Cap waggishly complemented me with my "recital" as he called it, and he knew all about music for he was an experienced clarinet player and he sure knew what was wrong with my talent. They all were good sports and there were no highbrows. We altogether had much fun. There were a lot of girls around and I was not that old to be bored with their company. To the contrary, I got the opportunity to acquit myself all right.

I also often went to see the basketball competition in the sports hall of the high school. Sports play a big part in American school life because it inclined the pupils to also do their best in the subjects of instruction. There was another thing. Boys who excelled in sports like baseball, basketball, football, and other athletics are assured of the popularity with both the boys and the girls. With respect to the latter, it seemed to me to be a nice privilege. The girls were rather reserved in their affections to boys and they were very critical as to their behavior. If you were not a match for their criticism, you were mere wind to them and you could just as well clear out. The American country girls and young women were not to be approached easily.

A young man like me at first had a hard time because he was an alien, a nonnaturalized foreigner. I just fell beyond their level. But since they had gotten to know me better and particularly when I got to work for the Accola family, I gradually got introduced. They no longer ignored me. Perhaps my playing mandolin may have contributed to it. Beside, I had some dough and was in the position to treat them on an ice cream or milk shake; a man like that seemed to be good in their books. Moreover, I could talk about things in the old country and from all over the world and also was able to chat about modern things as well. I had my own horse and was saving money to buy a car—a used car, of course! All this counted, not only for the young people, but also for the farmers themselves, and it was a reason for them to open their doors to me. When I was free I took part in many parties. Parties held by the neighbors, the Judges, who lived near Huxley, the Norings, the Söderströms, and many others.

On some day I determined to sell my horse and change her for a car. I sold her to a good man, but still it was a sad moment to me to see her go with someone else on her back. I had saved enough money to buy me a second hand car. I just wanted to follow the march of progress. I bought the old "tin lizzie" from Ralph, a cousin of Cap at Alleman, and I got it cheap. I only had to pay twenty-five dollars for it. It was an old unrigged Ford T-model.

I now was the owner of a "car." And since I could move faster than I was used to with my horse, I drove wherever I wanted to go in the least of time. More frequently I went to Des Moines and other places. Sometimes I went farther. One long weekend I even went as far as Nebraska—the "Beef State"—where I stopped in Omaha, the exact middle of the U.S.A. and the city where the immigration authorities had their head-quarters. I was pretty near to the lion's den. In the early trailing days, Omaha was the meat market for all of the western states. That was before Chicago gradually became the meat-supplying centrum of the country and even of the world. The state of Nebraska had the same vast cornfields as had Iowa.

Once in awhile I had my flivver overloaded with friends—on each fender in front and on the hind fenders and one inside behind me. It was great fun to drive in this way along the big paved roads like the Lincoln Highway and other motor roads. On Saturdays I often went to the barn dances that were held in the evening in Kelley, in a big barn, rented for that purpose. A great deal of the evening was spent with country dances. On a platform the fiddlers were seated, playing the Irish and Scottish ditties and tunes like "Turkey in the Straw" and "Flop-eared Mule." I really had a good time then.

One Saturday evening I was going to attend the barn dance again and I went for Bertha with whom I often danced. But I missed her because she wasn't home yet. Bertha was engaged with Thor Egemo, a nice fellow and very serious. Uncle Paul told me she and Thor would be at the barn dance all right. On my way back to Kelley I passed Lars Thorsten's farm. Brit happened to stand at the doorway and she waved at me. I yelled to her I'd like to know how Jörgen was making it at their farm, for I had not seen him in weeks. She yelled back he wasn't there any longer. I was kind of surprised and I stopped and drove my car into the yard. I wanted to know more about it. Her old man sat behind the window and waved at me. It occurred to me that Brit kept me off, but I insisted and again asked her what was the matter. "Come with me to the barn dance, Brit; then we can talk. And we'll have a good time too." "I do like to, Jerry," she said, "I think I've a lot to tell you about your friend. I'm convinced you don't approve with his ways and

I'm glad about that really. If you don't mind to be saddled up with me all evening, I'll go with you, though I'm not in the mood," she said. "I'd like to take you out with me anyway; you need not say much if you'd only tell me what Jörgen did to you."

She went inside, dressed up and we both went to Kelley. She admired my tin lizzie. "Gee, Jerry," she said, "this is swell. Wish you'd work for us," she added with a sigh. We had danced and sat nipping our grape juice for quite awhile. Then she said, "I never did like him. I was afraid of him. He's a crude guy. I don't know what he's up to. I can't imagine he's a friend of yours. He's a good-for-nothing guy. My dad fired him because he tried to become too familiar with me and also because he did not work the way he was expected to. Lots of times he did not show up in the weekends so I had to do the chores." I told her I had not seen him for weeks. "Where he works now?" I asked her. "He seems to live in Ames, but I don't know what he's doing. I believe he is involved in some unlawful doings. I don't know for sure. Anyway, he does not work on the farm any longer." "He'd made a mess of it," I thought. "He indeed was a sneaky dog." I had felt for long Jörgen would go that way. "Well, Brit, don't think of it anymore. Let's have a good time now. How are the parents about it? I know your mother did not like him the moment she saw him. He intimated to me he did not like her either and he said he cursed her. I never got deeper into the matter. The more I heard about him the more I gave him the wide berth. I haven't seen him for a long time. I wouldn't care if I did never see him again." We danced much that evening and we had a lot of fun. I took her home late in the evening and when I had opened the door to her I kissed her goodnight and went home. My new "car" took me there in no time.

I really could not say I got bored with my Iowan country life. If nothing was going on, neither in Kelley nor with the family, I often went to Ames or Des Moines shopping or to see a movie picture. Those "T" cars were a mass production of Ford. They were assembled automatically on the running belt. When driving them they were kind of noisy at high speed. Mine shimmied and shook in all of its joints, but it ran perfectly. I had to start it by turning an iron crank in front of the radiator. Beside it, a piece of wire stuck out of the radiator, which was connected with the choke. You had to pull at it before or while turning the crank, otherwise the motor would not start and you should not pull too long or the motor would be drowned.

As soon as the motor started, you had to take away your arm swiftly to prevent getting hurt by the stroke of the crank. When the motor gave signs that it was going to start and made a number of turns, you had to run to the drivers seat very quickly to pull up the gas handle, otherwise the motor would quit again. The gasoline tank was fixed under the drivers seat. The contents of gasoline in the tank could be measured with a little wooden stick. The steering wheel was on the left side. When you drew along the curb in wet weather, you had to jump out over the right side of the car to avoid the mud on the left side. Sometimes, when on our way, the motor stopped and refused flatly to start again. We, with combined efforts, put it on its hind end and pulled and wriggled at some nuts in its belly. Then it was let down and on it went again. I remember at the time we had our lift with Mr. Blackwell he told us the U.S.A. had about two million miles of traffic roads of which only ten thousand miles were paved. The Lincoln Highway, running from East to West, from coast to coast, belongs to the interstate highways. So does the Jefferson Highway, which runs from North to South. The former, America's first coast-to-coast auto road, however, was far from being a comfortable one all the way. In the Middle West states it might happen that in rainy weather you got stuck in the mud, the gumbo, as they called the sticky mire in Iowa and Nebraska. Many parts of the highways, though, were paved with tar and macadam and, apart from the mud roads, most of them consisted of gravel and stones. There were hardly any signs as to the directions and distances to towns. Only the main roads had route indicators.

All the same, twenty years before, in 1905, a transcontinental automobile trip was held from New York to San Francisco, which took 104 days because of so many impassable roads. The maximum speed of my car was about 40 miles an hour, so it did not take me long to reach Des Moines. Driving further west, past Des Moines, the Lincoln Highway crosses the Jefferson Highway. Between Ames and Des Moines there were only two gasoline pumps. Should it happen you stranded because you ran out of gas, you maybe could get some at a nearby farm provided the farmer was the owner of a car himself. If he was not, you were compelled to ask him for a horse to have your flivver pulled to the nearest filling station. It once happened to me. Most farmers still had their buggy, a cosy little carriage on four wheels, pulled by a horse.

The farmers around Kelley seemed to have taken it for granted that Jerry (that's me!) should permanently stay with the Accola family and marry one of the girls he knew. I loved my freedom too much, however, to get tied to the apron strings, even though I knew that marriage here would make me a citizen of the U.S.A. automatically. I felt myself too young and I wanted to be free to do what I liked. To be honest, in my secret heart I did not like farm work; this did not prevent me to do my job to the best of my ability. Cap had once thrown out a little fish as to what I thought of Lucy Caldwell. Lucy, a friendly young woman, had freckles and she was round. All the same, I guess she would make an excellent farmer's wife. Cap did not seem to know I felt affection for Dorothy. "Wouldn't Lucy be a nice girl for you, Jerry?" he asked me. I just felt what he was aiming at. It had become known to me that Cap possessed another little farm of about 180 acres, which he had leased to Harry Wills. Harry later proved to be a drunk. How he obtained the liquor in dry Iowa, no one knew. He could hardly make it himself, for you can't make whisky out of apple cider and he did not have a distillation outfit hidden somewhere. The possibility was apparent that someone supplied him with the booze at big pay, of course, because it was illegal. The habit of drinking too much had added more and more to his neglecting his farm, to great grief of his pretty wife, Maggy. She was often alone. They had no children to comfort her. I did not wonder about their childlessness, for alcoholism often leads to impotence. Maggy had to do most of the minor farm work, like the chores, cleaning the barn, and feeding the chickens. The heavy work was done by Harry the best he could under the circumstances. Once I had taken pity on her and helped Harry with picking his corn that looked miserable late in the season to get it in before it became too extremely cold. It appeared to me it was because of this awkward situation that Cap tried to find another tenant.

One Saturday evening I visited Harry and Meg to invite them to go with me to the barn dance at Kelley so they could cheer up a little, what would be fine to her. But again Harry was lying on his bed drunken as David's sow. Meg mentioned to me she'd seriously considered getting a divorce. "I'm leading a dog's life," she said downhearted. "I can't stand it any longer and I can't keep on managing the farm all by myself the way it ought to." She told me Jörgen Dahl had offered to help her with the heavy work. How he managed to have so much spare time since he lived at Ames puzzled me. But she said she rejected his offer, knowing very well what was behind his proposal. She confided to me she instinctively had an aversion at him. "I suspect he's the one who supplies the booze to Harry." What she said had struck me too, sometimes, but before Brit told me her story I'd never stopped at the thought he'd be that sneaky.

I very soon got knowledge of what really was the matter. A few days later Jörgen came to see me. He panted with fury when he told me of Meg's refusal to have him around her place any longer, in spite of his being on friendly terms with Harry. He accused me of conspiring against him, probably, as he said, "to have your way free with her." What he meant by this was quite clear to me. "What the hell you think you are?" he yelled, "you ain't her brother. When I'm around Harry won't touch the bottle." "Well," I returned, "he won't touch the bottle, I guess you will help him pour the liquor right into his throat. I'm fed up with you and your exploits." He made a row and it pretty near came to a fight in which I sure would have been worsted. At that moment Joe Roney got in through the gateway to talk to Cap about the thresher. But the family was not in. Jörgen thought it better to disappear, for Joe did not very much like him. He promised me he'd see me later. Joe told me it was an open secret that Jörgen had become a bootlegger. He seemed to work for a syndicate in Ames and he was supposed to earn big money on quite a number of booze addicts in this territory. Since he kicked that row, I never did see him again. It sure was a dreary end of our comradeship. I already had felt for a long time it would be going that way. It was a week later that I met Morris Noring, who told me he had heard Jörgen Dahl had taken refuge in Canada, having been chased out of the country on account of his bad record. How things ended with Harry and Meg did not become known to me. I believe Cap had given them notice.

My life on the farm went on quietly and without anymore incidents. I plowed, husked, and did all there was to do on a farm and before I was aware of it winter was there again—a winter with many odd jobs in the severe cold. In the winter of 1924-25 I was busy husking the last rows of cornstalks that remained in the fields. The temperature was 20° below zero. Having worked a couple of hours at a stretch—I nearly got finished—it felt like if I had no feeling in my fingers. I pulled off my mittens and saw my fingertips were black. They were frozen. I drove the horses home and ran into the house to warm my hands at the fire. But Cap dissuaded me heating my fingers and told me to go and get a bucket of snow from the outside and to grub with my fingers in the snow. "It's the only way to thaw your fingers, Jerry," he said. "And it will last hours till they are thawed." It indeed lasted four hours before they began to ache and got blue, red, and finally the original color. I lost a tip of one of my little fingers.

However cold it might be I drove my open car in all weathers to Kelley or Ames and my old flivver kept going all right. Except once. One day I returned home from Ames when I was caught in a heavy blizzard. Blizzards are awful cold snowstorms which originated from the cold wide plains of Northern Canada and sweep the open farmlands of the Middle West. I did not know anything about the fierceness of these storms and so I continued driving as long as I could, not aware of the great danger to stay in a blizzard till you got covered with the swept up snow dust. If you happened to get covered you could not get out and might freeze to death. My eyes got blinded with the fierce cold snow lashing me. I climbed out of my car just before it totally covered. As a matter of fact my car was stopped by the mountains of dry snow in front of it.

I was near Road 3 and I had to run for shelter and to keep moving to prevent freezing to death. The temperature must have been at least 20° below zero. I kept to the roadside as well as I could to keep out of the wind that cut my face. I came about the road where the farms were of Howard and Creighton. To reach Howard's place I had to stumble against the wind; to Creightons place I had the wind behind me. But I did not like to ask Creighton for shelter. I thought him an uncongenial guy, a big fellow with a smooth face, and I always felt ill at ease if I met him. I'd rather go to Howard and face the intense cold. I got hot coffee at the Howards. "When the wind drops I'll try to get through, Joe" I said to him. He was looking outside. "I don't think you'll get much chance, Jerry," he said. "You'd better stay here for the night." On a certain moment there was a lull and I ventured to get on my way home. I had to walk about two miles. With frozen ears and reddened eyes of the beating snowflakes I safely reached home. Next day I took a horse and a shovel to dig out my vehicle and pulled it home with one horse power.

In the spring, when the snow had gone, we again began plowing and planting. Cap mounted the tractor pulling the two-bottom plow and drawing deep furrows in the black brown soil. I, too, had to plow another part of the land. I had to do it with the horses. Afterwards we had to do the edging, and then the corn was planted. Suzy took care of her flock of chickens, Rhode Island Reds. The eggs were sold.

For the first time in my life I got to know how some animals were treated when they were up to being fattened. If it were a cock that was intended to be eaten, they searched for its midget testicles, which, when found, were cut loose with a sharp edged little knife. A bloody job! Most of all I remember the way the little boars—male pigs—were castrated. I was horrified to see how the piglets were pushed down and how with a sharp knife their little sack was cut open and the testicles ripped out. The little pigs then were released, upon which they ran away whining with pain. This, however, soon was over and they sniffed and rooted as ever before. This job was a mere necessity to the farmers and maybe they hated this operation just as much as anyone else. The worst job was to castrate the big old boars, hogs of 300 pounds and more. Those testicles had to be torn out with great force and the things themselves were as big as a fist and they had a steel-blue color. The boars had to be strapped to a post thoroughly to prevent kicking and bouncing. The least of tortures, I thought, was done to the hog that was to be slaughteed to provide for the winter meat provisions. One heavy blow with the hind end of the axe was enough to beat him unconscious. Immediately

116

Farmers keep themselves from riding in open cars. They have their Ford and Chevrolet sedans. Only some hired man happens to own an open flivver, bought with the little money he saved. There are not weather forecasts. In midwinter you can never predict whether a blizzard might show up. If it happens and you get stuck in mountains of dry snow with your open tin lizzie, you'll have to hurry for shelter.

---

thereupon a knife was stuck in its neck on the spot where precisely the big artery was and then the blood dropped into a bucket. From this the finest blood sausage was produced by the mistress. Then the whole hog was hoisted up and cut in nice pieces. Some of the finest pieces were consumed directly in the course of the coming days. The rest was salted and kept for later use. All parts of the hog were used. I found the salted meat delicious. On Thanksgiving, the national holiday of the United States of America, we ate turkey. We fattened and sacrificed one and we always ate too much.

Anyway, farm life had many facets, many I did and did not appreciate. So I lived through the spring the way I had done before. And then came the moment I seemed to be going the same dull round. Unrest came over me. I never was and would be a farmer; I had another background. I just wanted to get away to the world I was used to, not away from the Accola family, who had become my best friends. Far from that. Cap had treated me well and I very much liked him and I sure loved his wife Suzy. She, especially, was very dear to me. She never was cutting and she was always full of care for her family to which I, too, belonged. Cap was an honest, hard working man, human and merry, and the boys, Lowell and Glen, both were good pals.

No, it was not for that reason I wanted to leave. In my secret heart I disliked the tiresome farm work. Rising early in the morning, milking, pitching manure, husking corn, and tens of other odd jobs. You never were at liberty. I was town bred and longed for city life again. I wanted to go to Chicago and try to find a job similar to that of wireless operator, to go and sail if needs on a lake steamer. I knew there were special training courses to which I could enroll, for I had to have an American license for sailing on American ships.

On a certain day in May 1926 I gave notice to Cap. A month later I took leave and said goodbye. It was hard to leave the dear folks. Suzy had tears in her eyes and Cap did not say much. The boys cracked a joke and said they hoped to see me back soon; "that big city is good-for-nothing." I had sold my car for the same amount I had bought it for. And on that particular day I took my suitcase and left Rural Route 3 for Chicago, the "Windy City." Cap took me to the station with his car. On the Kelley depot I'd take the interurban to Des Moines, from where I should depart with the Illinois Central to Chicago. I took leave of Cap and with a lump in my throat I shook hands. I was glad the train was soon in. Cap watched me out. He waved at me till I couldn't see him any longer.

Chicago

March-September, 1926

I HAD NOT saved much money; I'd been stepping out quite often. I could afford, however, to pay my way for at least a month. First thing I did was to find a cheap hotel and, like before, I went to look for one in Dearborn Street. Chicago was known as the hobo capital—it swarmed with little hotel joints like that of the Bohemian at Cedar Rapids. By its position in the Middle West, Chicago had become a sort of tramp ward. Of all cities of the U.S.A. Chicago had the most furnished rooms to let. There were a lot of middle-class hotels just outside the Loop, close to the viaducts of the El. I found a cheap, decent hotel and obtained a small room on the second floor, scarcely furnished and with a single bed for the price of one dollar a night with breakfast. In the barroom downstairs I ran about the ads in the *Chicago Tribune* to see what kind of jobs might be available for me. I had to find work soonest possible, for I not only had to live but also had to save money to pay the fee for the radio course I intended to follow. I coped with the same difficulty with regard to what job would suit me, like was the case in New York, and finally decided to tackle the job of taxicab driver. This sort of work looked to me not only profitable but also interesting. Again, like for motorman in New York, I had to follow a short training which, in order to get qualified, should last no longer than a week. The advertisement was placed by the Yellow Cab Company, one of the biggest taxicab concerns of Chicago (and probably of the U.S.A.). They wanted drivers and driver apprentices who were to be contracted for at least one year after having been engaged. I decided to do it and next day I went to the office in East 21st Street to apply for the job of apprentice driver. After having qualified, apprentices were taken on as regular drivers.

Again, like in New York, there was a long file of candidates. First a medical inspection, followed by a technical test, and finally . . . a cap. Unlike the one of the streetcar business, this cap was a flat one. I obviously seemed to be condemned always to wear an uniform. Should I pass the final examination and be engaged, I was to be supplied with the dark grey cabdriver's suit.

I considered my dress as a sparks-wireless man to have been of a higher order, but what did it matter! I just earned money. The veneer of civilization was but very thin and it looked to me cabdriver was just as virtuous a profession as that of ship's captain. They both wore a cap and they both had to provide for the safe transport of human beings. There was only a gradual difference between the office of captain of a passenger ship on the high seas and that of cabdriver in the streets of Chicago. It was solely a question of preeducation. That of the former was very difficult and intricate and consequently, expressed in money, valued higher; that of the latter, less dignified and on a social lower level. The human and cultural aspects of both professions one should have to deliberate on, namely, whether the captain's cause looked more promising than that of the cabdriver. Both, however, were obliged to wear an uniform.

My first acquaintance with the beating heart of Chicago I made from behind the glass windows of the driver's cabin. Chicago, an enthralling town, a town of which the Middle West farmers say that it is not quite an American town but all the same awfully many-sided and fascinating. It is a town to which you love to belong to when you are used to be a resident of some little American town. My instructor, a little bulky fellow, Italian of birth, took his job seriously. This certainly was to my advantage, for I learned to become a careful and reliable driver. The jolting with my old "tin lizzie" in Kelley was just poor driving compared with the skilled professional driving I did with my comfortable modern car. These cars, and also my cab, no longer were started with a crank in front but had a kick-starter, a knob at the footboard that had to be kicked down, upon which the motor started.

Driving in the busy Loop district of the city took much of my attention and demanded much concentraton. My teacher was strictly attentive to my following up the traffic regulations. Not only the rules laid down by the public authorities had to be obeyed, but also those of the company had to be kept in mind. He insisted on my strictly obeying his manner of driving. I was not allowed to have my wheels touch the curbstones, not only for the sake of ensuring my passengers a comfortable ride, but also to spare the tires. I had to avoid shocks while clutching over to another speed, and I was to use my brakes carefully and efficiently. It was made clear that I always had to follow the directions of the traffic cops. Just the same I had to react quickly and drive steadily and fastly in order to deliver my passengers in time and safely at their place of destination. Moreover, I had to be polite and correct to anyone. As a matter of fact, this was in my own interest; "good service means good tips," my instructor said.

When I had a week of intensive training behind me I was invited to undergo two examinations: one for the city of Chicago and one for the State of Illinois. I passed these exams successfully and received my drivers licenses from the hands of an official: a bronze badge for Chicago and a silver one for the state. I pinned both badges upon the lapel of my uniform jacket. The uniform was given me in loan during the time I should be engaged with the company and I was under the obligaton to maintain it clean and in good condition. With my two license badges I was officially allowed to drive a car in all states and towns of the U.S.A. To me the main thing was that I could make me a living now I was appointed to the Yellow Cab Company as a finished driver.

Every day a cab was assigned to me with which I was supposed to transport as many customers as I could and to earn as much money for the company and for myself as I was able to. I was responsible for the right use of the car. I should look after and handle the automobile lent to me to the best of my ability and economize on the gasoline I got at the pump inside the garage. It was contracted that the company had the right to two-thirds of the receipts. The readings of the taximeter answered for the right amount. One-third of all receipts I could keep for myself. So I had no fixed wage, but the height of my earnings wholly depended on my ability to get as many passengers as I could. In other words, my achievement as a cabdriver defined the height of my earnings. The tips I naturally could keep for myself.

The first day already that I was released upon the public I got a rather unbelievable start. The first stand I took was at the Allerton Hotel on North Michigan Avenue, where I joined the file of cabs that stood there already. There were eight cabs.

They got their passengers in turn. As soon as the cab standing ahead got a load and drove out of the file, the cab that followed moved on. In this way every cab got its load.

While I stood leaning against my cab, waiting for the file to pull up, I had taken off my cap, for it was a hot day. At a given moment the hotel porter, doorman they called him, blew his whistle that meant a cab had to pull along the curb for passengers. The file did not move, however, and I looked what was the matter with the first cabs. The porter, trimmed with golden lace, kept on waving his arm and beckoned to someone. I did not quite gather to whom. Then, one of my fellow drivers yelled to me, "they want you," and to his mates he muttered, "they want the baby. Look at that. We can just as well quit standing here when they're going to pick from the row at random." I apologized but all the same pulled out of the file and drove to the hotel entrance. Two ladies stood there, looking in my direction. They obviously had set their mind on me. Why me . . . the Benjamin? Well, in this case it was not "gentlemen prefer blondes," but "ladies prefer blondes." They seemed to have preference for blonde drivers and I seemed to be the only blonde in the row. I got to exploit that!

The elder of the two was a resolute woman of medium age, friendly but explicit. The other one was an attractive dark-haired woman, thirty years of age, I guessed. The elder did the talking. "Drive us first to Madison Avenue, number 115, in the Loop." I was already acquainted with the Loop but so far had not driven there frequently, only once in awhile with my instructor. This would be my trial. All day long I drove them from one address to the other. They seemed to be engaged in the fashion branch, in fancy or gallantry goods or suchlike things. Buying ladies, I thought they were. I was as attentive as I could be for the two women and they seemed to appreciate this. Between twelve and one they went for lunch at the Walnut Grill in Randolph Street. I had to pick them up there at one. I drove to a street where I could park my cab and took my time to eat the sandwiches I had bought before I went to work—without coffee, for there was no coffee shop around and I couldn't nip out now.

About five in the afternoon they had finished their tour and I presented the account, having read the taximeter. They paid me, adding a royal tip. The elder woman paid, the younger added a sweet smile to it. This latter gilded the tip and made it even more acceptable to me. I thanked them correctly

The gold-burdened porters of the big hotels of Chicago have the appearance of generals. They, too, act as such. When calling a cab they blow the whistle and with a commanding motion of the right hand directs it to the curb. With his left hand, the palm opened upwards, he invites the guests to get in.

as I was taught to do. I had to keep polite to whatever client I had. A cabdriver had no own identity. He might be praised, he could be scolded, he should have to lump a rudeness and not give back an answer. He was a uniformed servant. He neither was allowed to get irritated nor was he to be affected some way or other by any amiable attitude of attractive women. As a matter of fact, he'd be a confounded fool to think the latter would ever buck with an occasional cabdriver. Keep all this in mind. You won't make any money when dreaming while you drive, I said to myself.

I wasn't quite sure of myself how to behave with respect to my colleagues like I did at the hotel and I therefore consulted them to know what they thought of it and what I was going to do next time. Shouldn't I have refused to get out of the file? They told me never to let pass a bit of good luck. They would probably have done the same. "Next week," the elderly woman had told me, "we are in Chicago again for a day and you should look out for us. You won't forget?" That second day I carried them all over the city and so I did in another three weeks. Together with the tips it yielded to me a lot of good bucks. But then I quit them. I wasn't married to them and I liked to change to some other area and extend my activities to the Loop and the railroad stations. The other guys might succeed me if they'd like to and I went to drive about crawling passengers. If I heard someone yelling "taxi!," I reacted immediately and in this way I got to practically every part of Chicago. Within a week I already knew all spots where cabdrivers could find their loads. I had to make long hours a day to catch as much money as I could.

I had never dreamt Chicago had so many aspects. Aspects, favorable in the sense of the many fine big buildings with nice lower fronts, especially on the "Magnificent Mile," the part of Michigan Avenue along the Loop on one side and along Lake Michigan on the other side. Aspects, unfavorable with respect to the slums in the near West Side. There were so many contracts in this big city the way I saw them that I could not say which was the most fascinating.

I had already driven my taxicab to the many stations in downtown Chicago; there were a great many. The railroads ran for the greater part underground. Not so long ago the trains used to ride at street level at several points in town. An outstanding example of railroad efficiency as to the transport of masses of people was the Union Station, quite new—it came ready in 1924. To this station I always had many customers. There were many other interesting parts. La Salle Street, for example, was the busiest street of the Loop, the financial centre of the city. Randolph and Monroe Street comprised the entertainment district with many theaters and restaurants. To reach these streets one always had to turn to the right; you were not allowed to turn to the left. Formerly, the Loop must have been kind of dirty with much thrash on the streets. Today the water sprinkler is ridden about the streets, cleaning the asphalt. I once slipped with my car on one of the smooth, wet asphalt roads. My passenger got scared to death, but I fairly well knew how to get out of a slip so I got my car almost at once under control. At the end of the trip he just paid me the fare he owed me—no more!

I had left the room in the little hotel where I stayed very soon after I got the job and had, via an advertisement, found room and board in East Huron Street with the Lennox family, Scots Canadians who had immigrated shortly after the war and had settled down in Chicago. Hugh was a carpenter and earned good money. They had a comfortable house with too many rooms. They rented one to me. Hugh came from the Scottish Lowlands while his wife, Mary, came from the Highlands. In that lousy war, Hugh said, he was gassed and had lost practically all of his hair—he had left only a couple of muttonchops at the sides of his head, which he coddled as if they were the only pets he had. He was too hard a fellow to get a syndrome of the dirtiness and bloodiness of the trenches, but when the war was over he had gained an addiction to the bottle to forget the four years of misery. His wife, Mary, understood him and soothed the mental wounds of the war by caring for him motherly and merrily. Jeanie, their daughter who had just graduated from high school and shortly started to work as a secretary in an office, loved her dad very dearly, while the little boy Jimmy still was going to school and did his best to be as agreeable as he could. It was hard for Hugh to get some liquor. He had to go to a speakeasy and it cost him a lot of money. Mainly for this reason he had taken me as a boarder in order to supply them with an extra income.

Hugh had a wartime friend, Bill Laerton. When he came to see Hugh, and he did so often, they always were singing. They then sang sensitive Scots songs. Jeanie accompanied them on the piano. When they sang the fine songs of Harry Lauder, the troubadour of Scotland. I soon was able to join in singing "Wee, Wee, Bonnie" at the top of my voice and when they came to "Roamin' in the Gloamin'" I was at my best. I did not perceive then that I won the heart of Jeanie with my singing. I had no idea in mind to make any advance to her; she was a bit younger than I—she was eighteen and I was twenty-five. We just had good times and often went to the beach for a swim, for the beach was quite near.

My work as a cab driver was too irregular to step out much. Jeanie had her work at the office all day and in the evening I mostly was too tired and stayed home. I also often took the night shift when something particular was going on in Chicago nightlife. This night shift was very tiresome to a greenhorn like me, although it was very interesting from the point of view of getting in touch with Chicagoan night birds.

In the night the streets were empty and lonesome, except that there were some cars speeding home and taxicabs transporting their blown-out loads. The stillness now and then was interrupted by the El thundering over the viaducts of the Loop. But very few people came out of the wayside stations. I rather got my passengers from the big railroad depots and the recreation centers in the downtown district—also, and most of all, from the speakeasies and dancings around Rush Street, Randolph Street, and Wabash Avenue.

Some passengers were easy going, without much ado or no faultfinders. Others, to the contrary, were chatterers who at the end had all kinds of bad remarks, especially when it came to paying the fare. But most of them were easy and gave royal tips. As I did not quite know all the streets in this big city and its environments, I sometimes had to bandy words with my passengers. One time I took a young man with his girl from Lake Street, corner of Canal Street, to West Ohio Street. I rode a long way under the viaduct of the Lake Street El, from where after awhile I had to turn to the right at Central Park Boulevard. The address was to be in this neighborhood on the left-hand side. The two were cuddling each other lustily. But if you might think they were altogether taken up with their courtship, you were mistaken. All at once the young man snarled to me: "Hey, you, what the hell you're going at, trying to double the fare. Turn to the left and next street again to the left. We're pretty near to Ohio Street." "Sorry," I said, "I did not intend to. I'm new here and ain't driven my cab this way earlier." All the same I got a good tip.

Driving through an empty city in the night had its hazards too, and one had to be exceptionally careful at street crossings. Many car drivers become inattentive because they think they've a free road of their own and take the corners with full gas. After my night work I used to sleep out in the morning and when it was Sunday I sometimes went to the Soldiers Stadium in the afternoon to see a baseball game. I also once saw a rodeo there. But most of all I went to Lake Michigan to have a swim.

To me the morning shift was most attractive. There was a bustle of a multitude of people going to the stations, the offices, and other undefined places. It was the best time for me to cruise for a load. They always wanted me to drive fastly: "Hurry-up, I'm late," or "Get on, I got to get that train." I had to watch, though, that I did not get in trouble with the traffic cops. The cop on the crossing of La Salle and Wabash already seemed to be down on me. As a matter of fact he was right, for twice already I had given his stop sign the cold shoulder. So far I had the luck I could avoid getting involved in trouble with the police. My instructor had warned me time and again that it was better to lose a tip than to get a summons.

And on that particular day, tresspassing for the third time, that particular cop waved me out of the traffic file and handed me a summons on which he had written I had to report at police headquarters at nine in the morning next day. There were more offenders of the traffic regulations, I noticed. We were ordered to sit down in what looked like school desks. In front of the "class" a sturdy sergeant with a long stick in his hand stood beside a blackboard eyeing us curiously. He then started to show us the various traffic signs "you have to imprint firmly into your head," he said. "You must bear in mind that you may drive in and through the Loop only straight ahead and to the right; never turn to the left," he taught us. "Outside the Loop you can drive in whatever direction you like." And to the violators of the traffic rules he said: "You are to get a jam when you don't obey the signs of the traffic police. See to it you do so in the future." At the end of his lecture he told us that our names were noted down and we got the warning that if we were summoned again we should be fined. "It will cost you ten bucks the second itme," the sergeant added.

We were allowed to go. I got off cheaply this time and sure watched myself against a repetition, although I thought noting down my name was not in my favor. The cop at the La Salle

Street crossing was again as friendly as ever. He became "Uncle Cop" again and we saluted each other like if nothing had ever happened.

I took variable shifts for I liked to know what was going on in a big city like Chicago during the time elapse of twenty-four hours. The intermediate duty was from 2:00 P.M. to 10:00 P.M.; the early duty, from 6:00 A.M. to 2:00 P.M.; and the late duty, from 10:00 P.M. to 6:00 A.M. One night coming home from my intermediate shift about 10:30 P.M., I found Hugh sitting in the kitchen with a big lump shining on his forehead while Mary was busy patting it with cold compresses. He had come home wholly upset, telling he had been robbed of all his money. I pondered about the amount. He never could have much money with him because he had been in the mood of drinking booze and could not have left much money. He had been attacked, that was a sure thing. He was leaped upon from behind, beaten down by a couple of young guys he said were Negroes. One of them filched him of his wallet with—as he said—ten bucks that were in it. He'd got the presence of mind to look at his assailants and where they fled and he was sure they'd disappeared behind the Allerton Hotel. "I'm gonna take the matter up to the police," I said to Hugh, who already had calmed down a little.

I first looked whether I saw a police officer patrolling; I did not see any. So I went to the nearest police station to tell about the holdup. Not long after, two detectives called to question Hugh. They asked him if he'd be well enough to go with them to the Allerton Hotel; maybe he could identify possible culprits should they be captured. I asked permission to accompany them so I could take care of Hugh. In reality it was because I thought it quite interesting to peep behind the curtain of crime. They consented, however, not before I had promised I should shield myself if it should come to a shooting party.

When we reached the hotel, they decided first to search the basement. One of the policemen went down the stone stairs beside the front entrance, the other took the back side. I went with the one who took the front. He knocked at the door and shouted, "Open up, police!" A Negro porter opened the door. Armed with a gun and a flashlight, he wriggled through the door opening and past the porter and I quickly followed him. We entered a dark passage. At the far distance I saw the flare of the torch of the other policeman. We were amazed to find so many side doors and as many dens fitted up along both sides of the passage. "I'd like you to open that door," the dick said to the porter. I saw a number of Negro boys standing beside a bed, looking frightened at the armed men. One of the dicks asked Hugh to identify: "Is it him?" "No, they were bigger," Hugh said. The following door opened showed the same scarcely furnished room—if one may give it that name. On we went, looking and asking. There were dens in which Negroes lied down on planken beds. They all were ordered to rise. "I don't recognize any of them," Hugh said, "but it was quite sure they were Negroes."

In one den a number of youngsters protested, but they were all the same ordered out with the guns. I plunged to a side and pressed myself against the wall. You never could know whether they were likely to shoot. "Is it him?" again the policemen asked Hugh. But Hugh was too honest a man to accuse at random. He was at a loss. He could not tell any of them had taken part in the assault. As a matter of fact it was possible neither of them had actually been involved in it. The policemen stopped their inquiries but assured us they would keep an eye on these surroundings.

It was a load from my mind none of these blacks had to do with the holdup. They sure would not keep living in these dungeons if they were not compelled to it. They seemed to be unable to go and live in a decent house, or perhaps they were too poor to pay for it. But this sure should not be a reason to suspect them of crimes they did not commit. These Negroes belonged to the black girdle of Chicago, comprising 100,000 Negroes, many of them living in the slums of South Chicago. Those in the basement of the hotel were housed like others under big buildings from sheer necessity. They resembled the old cave dwellers and I could hardly imagine such living quarters were to be maintained in a civilized country like the U.S.A. This way of living would only tend to promote crime. But it sure must have been a gold mine to the Negro porter, who on duty as a doorman was all smiles and attention to the guests of his hotel on street level. Below, in the dungeons, he catered for the black families housed in his domain and who had to pay him the rent and probably a big one at that! The policemen were sorry for this man, but the hotel management should have to be informed about what happened under its hotel. I had my doubt, however, as to the ignorance of the man.

It was my first encounter with crime in a big city. To the policemen this holdup was just a petty theft.

My next mixing up with crime in my capacity as a crawler was not long in coming. Crawling with my cab proved to me the most profitable way to earn good money. Every moment someone stood on the curb waving and calling "taxi!" In State Street and near the Loop I got most of my passengers. One morning I got a load at the Wacker Drive; a fellow who had to catch his train at Dearborn Station. It was, as he said, of great importance for him to get there in time. He only got ten minutes and he promised me a royal tip if I could manage to be there within seven minutes. Chance would have it that the traffic lights at the corner of State and Lake streets went green at the moment I drove to it, so I could keep my speed. Routine had taught me that when a green light turned on at the moment you were to pass you had a half-minute to pass the next traffic light. In this way you could quickly cover quite a long distance without being interrupted by other traffic lights. My calculation tallied and I reached Dearborn Station at Polk Street in record time. The results were a five dollar bill—one dollar seventy cents fare and three dollars thirty cents for me. On this passenger I earned a lot more than did my employer, although I had to drive with the utmost speed, risking a summons again or even an accident.

Crawling also brought me in close relation to crime I was not aware of. Whenever I went from Cicero or South Chicago to the Loop, I could bet my life I'd get one or more of those small illegal whisky traders in my cab. I vividly remembered what happened on that particular Tuesday in July 1926. I had just driven a client to Calumet Park in the southwest and drove back to reach State Street—to me this was always a good place to crawl for new customers. Near 126th Street in State Street I was hailed by two men, one of them carrying a heavy suitcase. They ordered me to drive to La Salle Street near to Harvard, where they told me to stop in front of a restaurant. One of the men got out, took the suitcase, and went into the restaurant. He returned with his suitcase after a quarter of an hour. Reflecting closer upon the doings of my passengers I came to the conclusion they must have been a couple of small bootleggers. These guys usually make use of a taxi to take their samples to their customers in an unobtrusive way. Most of the

The cab driver should not be too inquisitive when the cop made signs of recognition to the occupants of his taxi. You never could tell he later might thwart you, and you'd rather be friendly with shaky cops than get in trouble when you had given him away. And what of it! Only one bottle of real whisky is all he catches for turning around when the speakeasy is being supplied.

time they carried suitcases with them, fitted up for the transport of the samples of liquor they had to hand over. At the same time they also settled the accounts of the goods delivered to the restaurant owners. They consequently often carried a large amount of money with them.

The danger of my transporting these guys lied in the possibility that the antiliquor squad of the police, which stood under the supervision of Elliott Ness, was tipped and would chase them or that a rival gang felt itself waylaid by them and might try to violently force them out of their territory. I found this out when an ingrained senior cab driver had informed me about it. I kept on the alert, but on the other hand I earned a lot of bucks on them. And so I kept on driving them to their addresses.

One day I had a couple of guys who asked me to drive them to West Fullerton Avenue. There they ordered me to turn to the left and to proceed to a little park—I believe it was Black Hawk Park. I had to drive into it till I reached Metrill Avenue. At that moment I saw a cop coming my way, swinging his stick and looking conspicuously at my cab. "Just stop a moment," the elder of the two men said to me. The cop stuck his head through the opened rear window. In my mirror I saw they gave him a bottle of whisky, a flat one, a hip bottle, and the cop rapidly put it into his coat pocket. He said, "All right gentlem'n," and sternly looking at me, told me I could drive on. In my mirror I saw him quickly leaving the park swaying his stick. A moment later I had to stop again. One of the men got out and went to the restaurant that stood behind the bushes and when he came back he got in again and I drove them to Cicero. There I received my fare and an ample tip. With an impassive face I thanked them and turned my car to drive back to the Loop. That day my time was up and I had earned enough to quit the day.

Next morning I told my mates that I had the company of a couple of bootleggers all afternoon. They advised me to look into my back-sight mirror repeatedly to see whether they looked fearful. In this case a shooting party might not be out of the question. They tried to freeze out rival gangs by threatening them not too gently. "You'd better leave your cab then on the pretext you'd have to phone the company for some reason," they advised me.

I heard the strangest stories about the methods the gangsters used to safeguard their profitable interests. They did so by annihilating their competitors. To terrify the members of an opposing gang they once in awhile used to kill a leader in a horrible way. They tied a block of concrete to his feet or let him step into freshly made concrete, had this hardened, and then threw it in with their enemy fastened to it alive into a deep lake; he never was found. Most of the time the big bosses had their rivals shot to death by their racketeers whenever they got them cornered. These racketeers also saw to it that the owners of profitable joints paid their "protection money," their "grease," in time. If they did not, they were intimidated and eventually killed by them.

Among the police forces all over the world there always were shaky cops. And Chicago did not make an exception. There sure must be some cops who could be bribed and who screened the gangsters and who often took bribes from both sides—which was, besides getting a lot of money, also very dangerous. It was not easy to deal with this kind of guy. There were only a few crooked cops who were blameable for the daring attitude of certain criminal gangs. They had not been able to resist the temptation to earn this doubtful extra money. They did not actually take part in the bootlegging business and just turned round when something unusual happened or tipped their benefactors about possible movements of their rivals, which might have become known to them. But it sure was not a measure—a graduator—for the trustworthiness of the Chicagoan police force as a whole. To the contrary, the real cops were always present to defend the rights of the citizens and anyone who needed help could reckon on them. Lots of my passengers had as destination the region around South Wabash, Randolph, and Rush streets, where apparently most illicit liquor was to be gotten and the bootleggers had most of their big sales—the spots where most speakeasies, restaurants, and gambling joints were situated. In the speakeasies liquor was sold illegally over the counter. The booze often was of inferior quality. Sometimes the alcohol was mixed with essences. The costs of making a bottle of this stuff was about three dollars, and it was sold for thirty dollars. This sure was a very profitable business, but once in awhile someone lost his or her life when unsuspectingly using stuff that had been mixed with wood alcohol.

Many speakeasies were in the vicinity of the old nickelodeons. I often had people in my cab who had been to one of the many five-cents theaters—the so-called nickelodeons—where one could see a twenty-minutes movie show. Most of the outfits of these joints had been supplied by big mail order houses like Sears Roebuck or Montgomery Ward. The first one in particular was well known for its supplying small-scaled and relatively cheap film reels and apparatus. Many small bunglers set up such a nickelodeon and they even made some little profit with it too. In earlier days there must have been as many as some five hundred of these joints, most of them lodged in private houses, the lower front of which was changed and painted in a theatrical color. In 1926, when I was there, their number was gradually decreasing, owing to the fact that the quality of the little films became better and most of the showrooms bigger and more comfortable. All the same, in practically all nickelodeons illegal films were showed, films that were far from decent and were even pornographic. These films had been banned by the censor and now they were showed secretly, which naturally drew a lot of morbid public. Anyway these bungling little theaters—if you may use this word—were another interesting aspect of this big city.

One day I drove with three passengers on South Wabash Avenue, about number 3000, when I drifted into a razzia of the booze squad of Lieutenant Ness. At some point I was compelled to stop and at that moment my passengers seized the opportunity to jump out of my cab and beat a hasty retreat without paying me my fare. I guessed they must for some reason or other have been afraid to get mixed up with it. Since this raid most of the gangsters operating from this part of Chicago moved their trade to Cicero and to the outer sides of West Chicago in the vicinity of 22nd Avenue. It looked like the activity of the police was carried up, the more so as gangster chief Al Capone—state enemy number one—became even more daring. Colleagues of mine, better informed, told me police lieutenant Collins was on the warpath with him; the least offence of the Scarface would be sufficient to take him into custody. At the moment they were unable to charge him with anything. He lived like an exemplary citizen and carried on a furniture shop on Wabash Avenue perfectly legal. But it was an open secret that the members of his gang held council in his shop. When I worked in these parts of Chicago I transported birds of different feathers, women and men. This part of Wabash lied in a kind of notorious district; the slums were more around 13th Street in West Chicago. A typical phenomenon that struck me was that in the various restaurants women sat at the windows ostentatiously smoking cigarettes holding these in a long little pipe between thumb and forefinger and pointing their little fingers right up in the air—a sort of a gesture, showing their independence from the males. Well, in these restaurants, to be exact, illicit liquor was sold. These women, puffing their smoke, showed nothing was strange to them.

When the prohibition act—the Volstead Act—became effective in 1920, no one had the faintest idea what problems it would conjure. The more than 18,000 miles of frontier left ample room for a lucrative bootlegging business and for the side lines connected with it. One of the most extensive branches of the illegal liquor trade was the beer business. Many illegal breweries were established, mainly on the outskirts of the city. Small distilleries, everywhere hidden in practically unfindable spots, were a second source of income.

Rookie, an old cab driver, had me posted up to all things worth knowing. "For a cab driver," he said, "got to know what he could be confronted with. You know, Jerry," he said, "that

Volstead Act that had to take care of the observance of the prohibition laws never had a chance to suppress bootlegging. Look, there are only some two thousand tracing agents throughout the country who are principally dependent upon the aid from the side of that part of the population that favors the prohibition and of a number of official instances like the coast guard, the customs, and the immigration service. But in spite of this aid, practically no control seems to be possible. It might be able to function all right if they'd get the assistance from the man in the street. The latter, however, is more inclined to aid bootlegging because of the fact that he does like to get a drink once in awhile, even if it is booze or moonshine."

As a matter of fact, it seemed to me that everyone contributed to the smuggling and selling of liquor and so facilitated the activities of the gangs in making big profits, unaware of the fact that they indirectly contributed to the increasing crime wave. Even the municipalities that were supposed to act against speakeasies and other joints that gave rise to the gangsterdom were powerless. The officials had to cope with the general trend of things and they soon got infected, too, not to speak of their being intimidated, particularly by the newly created gangs. They were warned not to adopt too rigorous measures. There were also many forms of corruption among the custom-house officers and, curiously enough, lots of gangsters worked in the control services of the customs. Anyway, the hip bottle went from hand to hand. I had witnessed this with the cop in the park the other day.

Two days after I had the talk with Rookie, I became involved in a chase after a criminal by a detective. Leaving West Huron Street, where I had delivered a passenger and driving in the direction of the Loop, I decided to stop in Rush Street in front of one of the busy restaurants I usually caught some load. The moment I stopped there to take my stand, a checkered cab of another taxi company just left the curb and a fraction of second later a man darted out of the entrance and ran to my cab. He yelled to me, "Drive . . . hurry up." He tumbled inside. "Follow that cab, fast . . . faster, police," he shouted. He showed me his card. I speeded up and got sight of the cab in the distance before me, taking the bridge and turning to the Wacker Drive. The cab drove till La Salle Street and in the busy traffic of that street I lost sight of it. "Damned," said the dick behind me, "I got to get 'em, he's a murderer; set 'em up." I got to my highest speed and drove like a madman. I knew this neighborhood very well and I thought the cab must have turned to the right somewhere at Monroe Street. I was right. I indeed saw it driving in the direction of Union Station. This sure was one of the busiest parts of the city and I found it difficult to keep my eye on it. Maybe they did not see me from the side of the dogged cab; the driver obviously got instructions to shake off his pursuers. As far as I could see, he seemed not to have stopped at the station hall, for to reach the depot you first had to take a long, lowered passage. A moment later I saw the taxi coming out on the other side, while I was just going to drive into it from my side. As fast as I could I passed the station hall below and was just in time to see the cab turn to the left and disappear into Jackson Street. I got it in view again and I observed the cab had lessened speed. They apparently thought they'd shaken me off. I, too, slowed down a little. I now carefully maneuvered closer and closer, hindered by the traffic. The cab proceeded to State Street where you could make a left turn because it was outside the Loop. Then it drove ten blocks further into Randolph Street. I followed slowly till the corner to avoid they could see me. The traffic cop looked angry at me. I held up traffic. But when he perceived the man inside my cab who was frantically waving his arms to let us get through, visibly showing his card, he changed his temper. He knew the man inside and he understood what was going on.

The checkered cab now drove away from the Rialto theater. Its passenger must have gone into the theater. "Wait here," the dick ordered. I relaxed, took my ease, and kept looking at the entrance of the theater. I tried to form an idea as to how things would develop inside. The dick would show his card to the attendant and ask her where the man got seated who came in so hastily. If there was no seat near the man, he'd wait till there was one. In this case I had to wait for the dick quite awhile. But I was almost sure there was a seat free next to the man. The dick would take a seat beside the man. He then would stick his gun in the man's side, keep seated for a short while not to arouse consternation or panic, and after a few moments he would say: "Get up. Keep your hands where they are or I shoot. Get out quickly." He would force him out. The whole show would take only about ten minutes, I reflected. He ought to come out now, I expected. It lasted a couple of minutes more; then all at once they appeared. The dick pressed his captive to walk to my cab. "Get in," he said to the guy. He got seated behind him taking care to cover him with his gun. To me he

State Street, corner of Madison Avenue.
Here's where the cop regulates the
busiest traffic in the world. You can
even say busier than the corner 42nd
Street and 5th Avenue in New York. The
streetcar dominates and is swarmed by
taxicabs, yellow and checkered. Crossing the street you repeatedly get in a
person's way.

said, "to the police station South Racine," and he added, "number 100. You've made it. You're a good driver. At the police station, on the corner of Monroe Street, I delivered my load. The fare was three dollars and fifty cents. Still keeping his weapon in the side of the guy, he pulled a five dollar bill out of his coat pocket to pay me; I could keep the change.

Not long after this chase I met with another occurrence. Like I always did in crowded streets, I drove slowly along the sidewalk in State Street near Madison Avenue. This is the busiest part of the Loop and I never had to wait long for clients. Approaching Madison a car passed me, drove to the curb, and stopped in front of me. A man got out, left the car where it stood, hailed me, and jumped in. He ordered me to turn into Madison and continue to South Wabash. "Hurry boy," he said, looking back over his shoulder. It looked to me he was afraid of some car that was supposed to be after him. He urged me to drive as fast as I could and I didn't care to do so, although I kept a safety margin. I took the green light and drove to Wabash, about 22nd Street. He got out hurriedly, paid my fare with a royal tip, and was off like a lamplighter. I turned around to drive back from where I had come. When I had gone a hundred yards I heard the vicious rattle of a machine gun. I turned my head to hear where the sound came from and I suspected it came from about 22nd Street. I could not see what actually happened, but the feeling crept over me that it had to do with the man I had in my cab. I hastened to get farther away from what I thought must have been an assault or something like that and I did not like to get mixed up with it.

That evening I read in the *Chicago Tribune* there had been a shooting party in 20th Street. There were no casualties. So it might have been an intimidating row. A rival gang seemed to have tried to riddle the store of a member of another gang. Two detectives, who soon arrived at the spot, cleared the place. They were, however, unable to arrest any party involved.

In New York already I had heard that America was made dry, and I soon knew what booze was. Here in Chicago I actually saw what bootleggers were like and I was by virtue of my job prompted to get in touch with them anyhow. In Chicago the illicit liquor trade—the bootlegging-business—was dominated by gangsters belonging to different, rival gangs. There were three big rival gangs that fought each other with fire and sword. The notorious leader of the biggest gang was Al (Scarface) Capone, a very dexterous young scoundrel. Justice could not get hold of him because of his cunning exploits. His partner was the even more notorious Johnny Torrio, an older man, who led the gunning to settle the feuds between the gangs. The wickedest enemy of Capone and Torrio surely was Don O'Bannion, who owned most speakeasies and a number of big nickelodeons.

I was warned when I was in the neighborhood of speakeasies I should take in visitors and bootleggers alike and never give evidence of knowing of their activities. It was very well known among the cab drivers that Capone and Torrio had command of six to seven hundred racketeers and you could better have nothing to do with them, for they were armed to the teeth. Their pistols generally were hidden under their armpits, fastened with leather straps. These guys indeed were the scum of the scums. All Cicero was practically controlled by Capone and his confederates; his racketeers kept watch over more than a hundred bars and gambling joints. Don O'Bannion, their opponent, had a flower shop in South Chicago, somewhere near West 60th Street. Once I got sight of the "King of the bootleggers," Scarface Capone. He sat in an armored sedan with double-dick, apparently bullet-proof windows—a young man with a sly face and flabby cheeks. A second car, carrying his lifeguard, was following his. This man had become a multimillionaire from what he earned not only in the "ruby quarters," but also from the alcoholic drinks his organization sold to the common people, the workers like Hugh Lennox—little people who could not leave the bottle alone, feebleminded little guys who were tempted to enter the speakeasies where they had to pay an exceedingly high price for the booze. This latter was often tampered with. Many a druggist kept behind part of the alcohol meant to be used for medical purposes. They sold this part at a high price to the illegal distilleries of the gangs, which made "whisky" out of it, booze of the worst sort, which they again sold at soaring prices in addition. This rubbish was promptly disposed of. Much of the medical and industrial alcohol was diluted and mixed with some flavor. From one gallon they made three gallons or fifteen bottles of makeshift liquor, the bottles being provided with attractive labels. Cocktails cost about seventy-five cents. The racketeers demanded a high percentage of the profits on what was sold, which they collected once a month.

The year I came to Chicago, 1926, the competition between the gangs culminated in a bloody war, which was still going on in an obscure way. I was not quite aware of the dangers I was subjected to when driving my taxicab, coming at all times in all quarters of Chicago. Did I care? Chicago was so big; nothing would happen to me. I earned good money and I took whichever person to whatever place.

I wrote the folks in Iowa lots of times telling them how I was going on in Chicago and invited them to come and visit me, so I could show them the city. But Cap was unable to leave his farm alone and Lowell, the elder son, was absorbed in his high school exams. Glen was too young yet. A neighbor of them, Floyd, eldest son of the Söderströms, however, wrote me he would like to come and see me. "Maybe," he wrote, "we could make a trip on the Lake." Floyd's dad formerly used to take cattle to the stockyards but never had time to see the city itself. Floyd once had gone with him, but he neither had been far beyond the stockyards. If I would take him to interesting spots, he would take me to the stockyards to which he, as a cattle

The shores of Lake Michigan show many fine beaches. Michigan Harbor beach is one of them and you sure can amuse yourself there.

feeder, had admittance at all times. I thought it a pleasure to see him again.

On a certain day, soon after, Floyd knocked on the door of Mary Lennox's home. She made coffee for him and invited him to stay overnight. I had the morning duty and came home early in the afternoon. I was greatly surprised to see him that soon and hurriedly went back to the garage to ask a day off next day. And so that afternoon we first went to the stockyards, an immense collection of small corrals, separated by wooden fences, many of them crowded with cattle. At the far end, where the big funnels stood, they were driven by stock men out of the enclosures into a long pathway leading to the slaugh-

terhouse. When they entered it, they were driven into a narrow passage where they were killed by a shot in the forehead and moved further on a transport belt. Their transport on the belt was ended when they were hooked up and hoisted up and moved into the slaughterhouse. Successively they were cut open, emptied, and stripped of their hides. In a record of time a cow was metamorphosed from a living animal into a can of corned beef; the hogs in another factory, from a shrieking potbelly into canned ham and bacon. It was not very exciting to witness this process, but it was teachable, though I could imagine there were people who might have an aversion of eating even a bite of it if they'd been able to follow the process. I rather saw it from the viewpoint of to eat and to be eaten and I tastely consumed my hamburger and so did Floyd. Having visited the meat-packing plants of Swift and Armour, we took a taxi to Chicago harbor, where we booked for a trip on Lake Michigan next day. Floyd and I went that night to the Loop to see the nightlife and decided to end the day with a visit to the movies. Thanks to Mary's hospitality, Floyd could stay with us overnight. We made music that evening and sang a lot of songs together in which Jeanie assisted on the piano. I regretted Floyd had not taken his violin with him, for he was an excellent violinist.

Early next day we boarded the passenger steamer and after awhile passed the open Outer Drive bridge that gave admission to the Lake on our way to Michigan Harbor. We made a magnificent trip along the western shores of Lake Michigan.

Late that evening Floyd said goodbye and went back home again. He said he had had a terrific time. At the Union Station we shaked hands and parted. He had to travel all night and would arrive at Des Moines early in the morning.

Once, on the occasion of thanksgiving on the 4th of July, I went to the festive party of the Scots. I went with Hugh, Jimmy, and Jeanie to the Union Park where there was a big grassy carpet. Here the Highlanders gave a bagpipe and sword dance performance. Bill joined us later. Notwithstanding the colorful happening, the monotony of the bagpipe music after a couple of hours became too much for me. Jeanie, too, got fed up with it. We together went to the beach for a swim and afterwards had a dainty bite. That further afternoon we had a good time together. When we came home the others were there too. Before dinner we had time to sing a number of good songs at the piano. I had a jolly good boarding at the Lennox home and much diversity. Lots of times I did not go out and just stayed home to read the papers or a book. Mary's home sure was fitted up pleasantly, thanks to the care and the good taste of Jeanie. There were a whole lot of pretty things in it and on the walls; this just made it cosy. The house stood at East Huron Street, rather centrally situated with respect of the Loop and the Lake. I could easily and fastly reach my garage.

As soon as I got my driver's job I had myself matriculated as a student of the radio course at the Radio Institute, so as to get a training for the post of radio telegrapher on board American ships. The techniques were ancient history to me, although the appliances were new to me. They had been much improved. The membership fee amounted to twenty dollars a month; this included the training fee. So I had to work hard to earn as much as I could, because I also had to pay fifteen dollars a week for board and lodging at the Lennox home. Adding to this the money I spent on stepping out, I had to take a lot of rides to realize all this money. As to this latter, Chicago city comprised a territory that was preeminently suited to be worked by a taxicab concern like the Yellow Cab Company, and, naturally, by its drivers to earn their living.

Many of the customers I collected at the cultural Mecca— South Michigan Avenue—called the "Magnificent Mile." Good points also were Grant Park and the Art Institute about where Adams Street ends in the east, and not to forget the Academy of Fine Arts. Further, there were the big department stores from where I took quite a lot of people, especially when they had been shopping and carried their burdens of bargains. Many city dwellers were not in the possession of a car of themselves. Most common people went shopping in the big stores of Sears Roebuck and Montgomery Ward. Exclusive was Marshall Fields, which was more like a showplace of the city, and many people went there to treat themselves in the big tea and grillrooms. All of these giant stores were not only retail but also wholesale stores. The first two were well-known for their mail-order service. The mail-order catalogue or "wishbook" of these stores was suggestive for the taste of rural America. When I was with Cap I often turned over the leaves of this unwieldy catalogue. The one of Sears Roebuck contained no less than 500 pages and the ads in it comprised a number of articles as much as could be stored in all stores of a middle-sized town. I once had ordered, amongst others, a nice blue suit, stating my measures and the color I wanted. And it fitted me to a tee. From them I also got my macintosh and my shoes and high boots. Most farmers I knew, however, bought at Montgomery Ward, maybe because in the beginning, when it started with its mail-order business, Montgomery Ward had installed a commission of Iowan farmers at the time to make inquiries as to the quality of its articles. On account of the results, MW had gained the confidence of most farm people. In these big stores one could buy anything one wanted from a box of pins to a precut balloon-framed house.

Chicago, I thought, had perhaps the most stores and shops of all big cities in the world, New York included. In the heart of the city—the Loop—there sure must have been more than twenty shopping centers. Altogether Chicago must possess ten thousands of shops and stores. At least four or five times a day I had to take my customers to the Furniture Mart and take them back. This Mart had been opened recently at the Lake Shore Drive on an unique place at Lake Michigan. It was known to be the biggest furniture store in the world, retail as well as wholesale.

The passengers I took to Evanston mostly belonged to the better situated inhabitants. Coming from the Loop I had to drive through what formerly used to be 12th Street to reach the lake front; now it was linked together to one Lake Shore Drive. The authorities had worked on the shoreline plan for years. The results were that you now could drive straight on from Michigan Avenue along the lake to Evanston. This, too, was made easier by the recent completion of the Wacker Drive, which now formed a magnificent connection between the Loop and the Outer Drive.

Actually the Chicago streets had gradually been dislocated by the increasing car traffic. As to the Loop, the authorities had been taking measures to prevent traffic jams and inside the Loop drivers had to turn to the right in order to get to some block. On account of the increasing number of automobiles, which made living here impossible, the heart of the city by this time mainly was composed of banks, business houses, and stores. The residential quarters had moved outside the city. The West Side is for the greater part inhabited by the lower class, the houses and apartments of which look kind of disconsolate. This is mainly due to the fact that the dwellings are diversified by second-hand shops and small factories. On the outskirts are the suburbs where the middle and upper class live. The elite, the rich people, have their country houses and expensive flats in the north, in Evanston. Their children attend the colleges and universities. The rich do not buy on terms; the middle and lower class do and especially the latter lives from hand to mouth.

According to my fresh knowledge of the city of Chicago in my function of taxicab driver, State Street was the leading retail store street; La Salle Street, the financial centre; South Dearborn, the office quarter; and Randolph, Monroe, and North Dearborn Streets the entertainment district with many theaters, motion picture shows, and restaurants. On my rides through Chicago I often drove past the regions where most descendants of the Dutch lived. In broad outline you could say the Dutch "colony" lived near to the west of Michigan Avenue, about from 103rd to 113th Street and in the neighborhood of Halsted to the west. There were also some other quarters about Loomis and Lincoln Street, Van Buren Street, 18th Street, and further in west Chicago near Oak Park.

One evening in July I went to a popular concert given by the Chicago Symphony Orchestra in the International Amphitheater on the corner of South Halsted Street and 43rd Street. It costed fifty cents. I heard the "Hungarian Rhapsody" of Liszt, the "Peer Gynt Suite Number I" of Grieg, and a little piece of modern music I don't know anymore what it was. This pop concert was meant for the common people who neither had the opportunity nor the money to go to an expensive classic concert in one of the big concert halls. As far as I knew about it, there had been a number of music lovers who had the idea to have also those people not blessed with worldly goods—the lowest paid, the laborers—enjoy classic music. For this purpose they stimulated the execution of cheap concerts, which drew quite a lot of people. In this way they also made it possible for me to transport lots of people to and fro. And the Chicagoan taxis were not expensive.

Not so far from the Loop with its fine shops and its prosperous bustle, Chicago also had its slums. In earlier days these poor quarters were built around the factories, which is the case in almost all big cities to make it possible for them to easily attract the necessary labor forces. Particularly in the near West Side, along Halsted Street, you could still find demolished and condemned dwellings, some of them giving shelter to the homeless. This, however, was exemplary. Most of the people now, to a certain extent, live in reasonable houses.

A few miles to the south of these quarters you came in the vicinity of the stockyards, the "Packingtown" as it was called, which town surrounded the meat-packing factories; there, too, were many slums. Formerly, crime ran riot in these quarters

Chicagoan musical life is known all over the world. No wonder Chicago has a great number of conservatories. The education often culminates in a performance in the beautiful Orchestra Hall on South Michigan, the home of the Chicago Symphony Orchestra.

and alcoholism was hard up. After the proclamation of the prohibition laws the latter flowed back and moved to the more fashionable places—to the Loop, Randolph Street, Rush Street, and other places with many restaurants. Chicago, indeed, was the center of the "booze belt," dominated by Capone's speakeasies and the grog shops in the many parks.

In the West Side more was done for the social improvement of its inhabitants. Recreation and welfare work particularly had a wholesome influence on the conduct of the people of the slums. A crusade was unchained against illegal alcoholism, which culminated in the forming of the Women's Christian Temperance Union. This Union built in 1906 the Women's Temple in Evanston, the part of Chicago that was made dry earlier already. Well-known champions for the human rights and for social welfare like Jane Addams and Ellen Gates Starr bought the former residence of the late Charles J. Hull and fitted it up as an asylum for the poor and the homeless. They called it the Hull House and this became the most noted building of the brilliant city of Chicago. Later a kindergarten was added to it and up at the moment when I saw it for the first time, it was a complex of a dozen buildings. From these the humanitarian work was carried out. Even now the slums themselves had vanished for the greater part. At the time I drove my cab to these neighborhoods, festivities were organized, film and dance evenings were held as a means to combat the influence of the saloons, the speakeasies and the nickelodeons; and of these, there were still many in the northwest side. There were all kinds of activities going on in the Hull House and I often had passengers to and from South Halsted Street. There was every reason to take it for granted that in the gay twenties Chicago was leading in dispersing social reform movements throughout the Middle West and even throughout the country. Chicago's location in the middle of the network of the big railroads made it the center of these activities.

My garage was pretty near to the West Side. It was situated in West Huron Street and driving west you came to the north branch of the Chicago River. This river with its five drawbridges connects the north side of the town with the busy Wacker Drive, dominated by the white Wrigley Building, the Tribune Tower, and the London Guarantee Building—the latter situated on the spot where in the olden days Fort Dearborn was located. Via these bridges you can reach all places in the city, places which to me as a cab driver were important. When I had to take someone from here to the vegetable market, I could directly drive to West Randolph, where the big marketplace is to which the vegetables in first instance are conveyed to be distributed later. Two blocks further to the south is West Madison Street, the newspaper center, with many little eat houses and ice-cream bars. The corner of Madison and State Street was the busiest corner of the world; I thought busier than the corner of 5th Avenue and 42nd Street in New York. Often I had to take passengers to the Furniture Mart near the Navy Pier and countless times I drove on Michigan Avenue to the south of which you come to the "Magnificent Mile," one of the finest boulevards of the world. To the north you can drive a great number of miles at a stretch along Lake Michigan with its vast beach. I often went to have a swim with Jeanie on the beach near Oak Street. Further to the north lies Evanston, the fashionable district, where about the Northwestern University is located.

When I had the night shift I nearly always used to drive around the Loop under the extensive viaducts of the El, which encircles this crowded city heart. Following these viaducts, above which the trains thunder, you can easily find the streets you wish to reach. It did facilitate my gathering knowledge of the street plan a whole lot and the first time I was new here I sure learned the situation of the streets very fast.

The railroad stations played a prominent part in my sphere of action. More than once I took my passengers to Dearborn Station, via Dearborn Street, one of the best known and busiest streets of Chicago. And once in awhile I had to move people further on South Dearborn Street to South Chicago, the industrial territory with its steel mills and, of course, its slums. Back from the South Side you can drive along Grant Park, the biggest park of Chicago with many nice buildings and musea. On summer evenings they occasionally have music events in the open and also big expositions are held there. More to the north of it lies the giant Soldier Stadium, in which some fine football and baseball games are to be seen and once in awhile a rodeo, for Chicago used to be the "cowtown" in the early cowboy times. The surroundings of the Soldier Field are magnificent. North of the city, in North Side Park, another baseball field is situated, the field where the "Cubs" play. Chicago displays so many variations of life that it is hardly possible to mention them all—the Zoo in the suburb, Brookfield; Rush Street with its nightclubs; Jackson Park with

The El stations are not to be thought
away from the local scenery of Chicago. They perform an essential part in
traffic and they form a link between
the town districts and the vast expanse
of Greater Chicago. This here is the
station at Wells and Quincy streets.
When you walk down the street, passing underneath, you come to the Chicago River.

the Museum of Science and Industry. And so, anyway, I thought Chicago the finest town I'd ever lived in.

And then, some day something happened that I'll never forget all my life. I was just busy in the garage filling the gasoline tank of my cab when I was tapped on my shoulder. I turned around and faced a man dressed in an uniform, wearing a cap that made me think of a cop; but it was, like his whole dress, khaki colored.

He looked at me closely, without saying a word. A feeling of approaching mischief crept over me—of an omen that would determine my future fate. "Are you Gerard Leeflang?" he asked me. "That's me," I answered with bated breath. "Well, then, you'll have to come with me," he said.

Old Birch, the garage chief paced to and fro behind us. "Sorry, Jerry, I'm so sorry," he called at me, "I couldn't help, I had to tell him. He's from the immigration, buddy," he added. "Yes," the man said, "I am an officer of immigration and I must take you into custody for violating the immigration law." He made a gesture with his right arm as if he wanted to say "follow me." There was something of insistence in his look that compelled me not to resist his invitation to follow up his order. We stepped into a cab. Now, in my turn, I was the passenger. But what sort of a passenger!

I looked back to the garage entrance and saw Ole and other men look after me with compassion. They were good men. I worked with them in very friendly cooperation and my sudden departure seemed to have shocked them utterly. Our taxicab drove from West Huron Street to Dearborn Street and followed this street till Illinois Street, where we got out in front of a gloomy building. I read the plate above the door— Cook County Jail. It turned my stomach and I felt my face got set with misery. Cast into prison. Gosh, this was the last thing I'd ever thought of!

The officer was correct but relentless. "I know I was wrong, sir," I said to him, "but to put me in jail for it, I sure do not deserve this. I have behaved myself like any decent American citizen." "I'm sorry for you, buddy," he said, "but I have to do my duty."

The man's face was ascetic without any trace of emotion and I wondered why maintaining the law should always be coupled with callousness. If this man had not solely treated me as an object of lawlessness but, instead, had added a tinge of human feeling to it and had put some heart in me, however little, I should have resigned to my ill fate with more courage. He might at least have told me that I was not considered to be a state enemy and that I had only been placed under arrrest for a short time until my expulsion. A fellow prisoner afterwards told me about this latter. The immigration man pulled at an iron knob and I heard a bell ringing loudly. The door was opened by a dark-haired man with a white face, wearing a cap and a sweater that looked as gray as he himself. With a number of compliments and a few words I was given in charge of a guard, who came to me. The immigration man went out and I never saw him back again. In my heart I cursed him for his sitting mum all the time.

The man in the gray uniform, a guard, I presumed, took me with him to a dingy little room where I was led before another man with just as white a face as the other—a short, broad-shouldered man with a mafia face, seated on the other side of a table. He invited me to empty my pockets and I had to put the contents upon the table. This man apparently had been doing his work for quite awhile already. He must have been an inmate of this jail, himself a prisoner, obviously with prolonged imprisonment, who had been granted this job on account of good conduct. The way he took my hand to make fingerprints pointed to his routine. He grasped my right hand, pressed my fingertips on a wet ink pad, and next on a sheet of paper. "Now," I thought, "I am registered in the annals of the American justice and considered an offender of the laws of the U.S.A." I felt sick about it, but it did not seem to bother the two men. I was no longer a human being. I was an object, a thing, a number.

"Follow me," the guard said to me, "I'll show you your lodgings." It sounded like it was not quite without a tinge of humor the way he said it. The agony on my face seemed to have inspired him to his hangman's humor. As a matter of fact, this was all he said. We went through a long barred pathway with on both sides cells in which prisoners were looking at me curiously and sometimes shouting at us. What they cried I could not quite gather because I was too much occupied by what was going to happen to me. Halfway the long latticed passage the guard stopped, took a key from his bunch of keys, and opened a cell in which were already two men. "This is just temporary," the guard said, "we'll put you somewhere else later on," and he slammed the grated door behind me. He went away leaving me dazed and terribly unhappy. It sure was an ill-fated day.

I looked at my two fellow prisoners, an old man and a young one. The young man immediately started conversation. "I'm Heevey," he said. He did not stick out his hand. Shaking hands was a mockery in this situation. "What they've picked you for?" he informed. "Illegally entering the U.S.A." "Oh, well, then they won't keep you here long. They put you on a boat back to where you came from," he said. "I'm a dope fiend," he continued, "cocaine. They've caught me for swindling." He showed me his thin white arms, pulling up his sleeves—arms full of red scratches and blue stains. "If I take snow, I can see where and how I can forge signatures and grab money by means of dud checks. This is the fourth time they jail me and I do it again and again. I ain't got the vigor to kick off. I'm always in want of money and then I have to get it somewhere and go to doping again," he said, disheartened. "And the old man here, too, is a regular customer." "Yes," the old man spoke, "I'll be blowed if I'd ever pay the alimony to her. And if I don't, they every time put me to jail again. That woman, I hate her like poison. She won't get a dime. After some time of imprisonment they have to let me go. I promise to find work before a pre-arranged date and pay the alimony. Then all the same happens again and again: no work, no pay, wife to police, police takes me to jail."

I sure had landed between a pack of wrecked bums. The air of the cell nearly choked me. I was not far from getting claustrophobia and in utter disdain sank down upon one of the planken beds.

A few hours later an old warder came to take me out and to what he called a permanent cell of my own, where I could recover from my emotions. The cell was situated in the middle of a passage along the bull pen—a big square where twice a day the prisoners were aired and where they had some more elbow room. My cell was provided with a privy—if one may call it that way—a stinking, dirty, yellowish white bucket with a cover on it; further, there was a plank bed with a mattress and a blanket. I had to stay in my cell for the rest of the day and was not allowed to get aired in the bull pen. At nine the lights were turned off and everyone had to go to bed. From the bull pen some light penetrated the darkness and so I could see vaguely my surroundings. The privy was conspicious. I threw myself on the bed to calm down and tried to sleep in spite of my misery.

Not long after I had myself laid down on the bed I got a terrible itching in my neck and when I scratched behind my ears I noticed something living escaped from under my fingertips and I felt something dampy. I scratched on different places and every time I felt a moving object. I smelled at my fingers and sniffed the stench of dirty almonds.

"Bugs!" I yelled. But nobody heard me. When I laid down motionless for a moment I felt like if drops of water hit my face; the drops were dry, though. And then I understood what was the case. My cell was infected with bugs. This vermin apparently had not had any victims for some time and was more bloodthirsty than the wildest beasts of prey. In battle array the bugs walked along the walls in the direction of the ceiling from where they pounced upon me. It was horrible!

I yelled and howled and beat the iron bars with the heels of my shoes to arouse the warder. After a while the old warder came with a flashlight to ask, "What the hell all that noise meant to be?" "Bugs," I cried, "they're eating me. This is monstrous." "All right, all right," he said, went away, and soon returned carrying a spout with destructive chemicals. "Here," he said, "take this. When you spout they'll keep away. Tomorrow you get another cell." And off he went. I heard him grouse, loudly: "Rubbish heap here. It is high time they build a new clink." I spouted like a mad man. But some of the devils managed to get through and still attacked me.

It was an endless nightmare. This cell was a torture room. Hunting the voracious little monsters kept me awake all night. The dirty almonds smell was unbearable. I cursed the prison authorities who tolerated conditions like these. Perhaps they knew nothing about what was amiss inside their old prison. Anyhow, in a friendly town like Chicago, from which I knew by experience that it was one of the most habitable cities of the U.S.A., it was unconceivable that they should tolerate a state of things like in this Cook County Jail. In a civilized world prisoners were no longer tortured and I took it for granted that in this America, preminently the country of freedom and humanity, conditions of this sort should have aroused a wave of indignation, should it become known. And it sure would be the case if they knew it was to happen to a light defaulter like me. Every time I smelled the almonds scent I got sick and got to hang over the privy trying to vomit. If this was the punishment of my offence—to enter the U.S.A. illegally—there would be no judge who could punish me more severely.

At daybreak, when I could clearly see the walls, I saw the last columns of bugs marching in two, three rows, disappear via a black seam in the ceiling, making themselves ready for the following night operation. To my great relief I was removed that morning to another cell on the second floor.

At ten o'clock I was with the other prisoners admitted to the bull pen. Sick at heart, I sank down on a ridge halfway to the cell passage. Tens of prisoners talking together shuffled about under the watchful eyes of a warder. One of the men came to sit down beside me, a decent guy at first sight. He formally introduced himself, which made me fancy myself to be again in the civilized world. "Jim Roberts," he said, "I'm English. What'd you be here for?" "I jumped ship and entered the U.S.A. illegally on my seaman's pass," I answered. "Now they caught me, after more than three years. It's very hard to me to leave now." "I daresay. But you're a lucky dog. It's just a couple of days in this dirty joint; they'll put you on a ship bound for where you came from. You're not English, though you talk English correctly." "No, I'm Dutch." We paused awhile. Then I said: "It's a hell of a place here. Last night they put me into a cell in which the bugs marched off with me. I was desperate. I'd never before been in jail in my life and I was totally upset and at a loss what happened to me." "Oh yes," he affirmed, "that's the notorious cell for the newcomers," he said, and he continued, "they put 'em in there in order to keep them tight, to keep 'em in hand," he emphasized.

"What you're here for?" I asked him in turn. "I knocked down a fellar who tried to get hold of my wallet. I hit him so badly he landed in the hospital . . . and I, in prison. I am indicted for heavy maltreatment and am waiting for the verdict for two weeks already. Tomorrow I must appear in court." "I hope you have good luck," I said. "A rotten set here," he continued. "Too small for so big a crowd of prisoners. It stinks here and they make no distinction between one and another. Hardened criminals and murders can associate with light cases, like you. They have you aired in a bull pen where repeatedly the condemned are hanged. You see that trap door there above in the middle of the wall?," he pointed up at a square hatch, fitted in the wall, "that's the drop of the hangman. It opens downward. He who is condemned to be hanged by the neck must stand on it with his neck in the halter and on a given sign and at a fixed time the hatch is loosened and he flings down." We remained speechless for a few moments. Then he continued, "They told me the victim keeps on struggling and for a moment keeps alive and then bulges out flabbily—dead!"

I glanced upwards horror-stricken. "Often the condemned person waits for months, sometimes for years, before execution takes place. This is no judgment; it is sadism, regulated murder. I would call it a legal vendetta. The criminal should be sentenced right away when guilt is proved. But if there is only the slightest doubt as to the guilt and the jury can't come to unity right away about the evidence, the death penalty should not be carried out." After this elongated tirade he gloomy gazed to some undefined spot. "What will become of me, I don't know," he sighed. "You sure are better off; they'll release you soon."

That afternoon one of the warders took me out of my cell and gave me a broom. "You may sweep the floor in the lower passage. Tomorrow you can also sweep the bull pens and on the upper floor the murderers row," he made clear to me. I swept all afternoon and got to the second floor. Near the entrance door there were a number of cells the interior of which looked different from the cell I was clapped in. In the cell to my left hand a gaunt little man of about forty stood behind the bars looking at me with extinguished eyes. He hardly seemed to see me. In the cell to his right a young man of eighteen or nineteen years old, with red hair and freckles, sat down, his hand under his chin. He looked up when I came around and glanced at me so despairingly that it shocked me. "These cells differ from those I'm lodged in," I said without any harm, "Where you're jailed for?" There was a silence for some minutes. I neither did say a word for I was scared by the stiffled face of the young man. Then the old man said: "We are condemned to death. My God, I wished it was done with me. This waiting makes me insane." The man stood there, his hand clenching the bars. His face was puffy and yellowish pallid; it had no expression. Only when he raised his eyes and looked at me I saw in it an immense agony. To me it was a terrifying moment. I got scared with the distress that suddenly lied on his face. The young man did not move but with his chin in his hand he crooned, "They hang me for one moment of passion. I had no intention to hurt and all evidence is against me." All at once he yelled, "Get me out! Get me out!" He then relapsed into silence and sat down more apathetic than ever.

The old man went on: "the Salvation Army comes this afternoon again, but they can't tell me a thing. I have to straighten it out by myself. I killed my wife. I shouldn't have had it come that far. I hated her. But the dirty fellow who came between us walks at liberty around this jail." Again his eyes showed mortal anguish. "I'm afraid. They kill me like a rat. They keep on killing, they take revenge on those who took revenge. It goes on and on. Wish, by God, I shouldn't have done it."

Bob had told me the whole story of the hanging of "Pretty" Floyd Cummings. He had heard it from the mouth of Warder Peterson. He watched Floyd die. "There were more than ten eyewitnesses among whom a number of reporters. One of them fainted when the man fell and died; he'd never before seen someone die that way. Behind that trapdoor over there was the gallows itself with the pale noose fastened to the crossbeam. Peterson told me about it. The hangman stood behind on a perch on the platform above the ten steps the condemned had to climb to reach the platform. The hangman was anonymous. He got an extra salary for doing this gruesome job. Chaplains or domini always climbed the steps beside the condemned, saying prayers and asking the Lord to have mercy on the poor wretch's soul: the Lord giveth, the Lord taketh away. Than that trapdoor over there opened and there he hung for more than a quarter of an hour. Then the doctor declared him dead. They told me they don't feel nothing, but the warder, who stood very near, heard him gasp for breath before he dropped."

The old man looked at the red-haired young man in the cell beside his and began again to stare before him. I went on with my work and dared not look again into the cells. It made me nervous and I was very near to getting an attack of claustrophobia again. It was a good thing when the guard called me for some trifling job and he then ordered me to my cell again.

In utmost distress I had written a letter to Cap to tell him about my misfortune and begged him to get me out some way or other. He could be able to testify as to my behavior. I had requested the warder to have my letter posted, which he had agreed to. I was impatient for liberty and hoped Cap would do something in my behalf.

Next morning at ten o'clock airing I was ordered to sweep

on the third story. As I already knew, on this floor were the cells and the little bull pen of the grave criminals, there was what they called the "murderers row." I also had to sweep the cells of the prisoners. It was altogether a rough gang that crowded this bull pen, although there were a few men who looked to me to be of a better standard. They left me go on quietly, but once in awhile I heard remarks like "A guy who'd buttered the guards up to get free air." A tall young man with a pleasant face every now and then pulled them up if they became to play rough. I just pretended not to hear them sneering and I imperturbably swept on and on. I had quite much sweeping work in cleaning the cell of one Christianson, a big guy from Swedish origin, to judge by his name. He had the appearance of a villain, had a mean face and a sinister grin. He suddenly entered his cell and grab me by the throat "I'm gonna kill ye," he hissed, "then you'll be in hell before I get there." He tried to strangle me. In a fraction of a second I reminded me the time that as a member of the athletic club I took part in a wrestling competition and had myself thrown forward to get rid of my opponent. I now applied the same trick; he lost his hold on me. With a sardonic laugh he renewed his attack.

At that moment the other prisoners overpowered him, shouting, "Cut that out; leave 'em alone." Three men tugged him out of the cell, while the warder came to rescue me. Christianson panted and tried to wrench himself free. "I'll get that sunnerverbits another time," he shrieked. It looked like he had all the hate he fostered against society discharged on me. I stood trembling on my legs, beyond my wits what to do. Then the guard took me back to my cell. After this racket I needed not to sweep on the murderers row anymore because I thought the guards were afraid of a new hubbub and they seemed to be powerless against this riffraff.

Anyway, I had already witnessed quite a number of touches of evil in human nature since I was in custody. I could imagine those guys, waiting for their death in this nauseating sphere, sometimes got in a mad fit. Most of them were condemned to death and they did sturdy to suppress their agony. I am sure, however, that among them there were more guys like Christianson, who would not shrink from killing someone just for the fun of doing it. My knowledge to fathom the human attribute of being able to commit crimes without any motivation whatever had by this time been firmly enrich- ed, though seeing the acts of the men who had rescued me, I was confirmed in my belief that on one side, human beings were loaded with vice, on the other side, had pity on their fellow creatures. In this damned jail I had to keep on the alert, and I became more reactive then ever before.

Of all experiences I had in this Cook County Jail, the climax came next evening. About nine o'clock on that evening jail life was startled by a heavy explosion somewhere in the rear of the old building on the ground floor. In the choking atmosphere, behind bars with no escaping possible, I broke into cold sweat. I lied down on my bed and resigned to whatever calamity was impending over me now again. I was waiting for the fire that would follow an explosion. But it did not happen.

Next day I heard Red Ferret, a notorious gangster, who was locked in for bank robbery and who had his cell in the rear end of the jail, had tried to escape with the assistance of his accomplices outside. They had placed a bomb against the outer wall in Illinois Street. The hole it made, however, was too small even for little Ferret to get through, so he had had no chance to get out in time. "Red" Ferret was a small, pock-pitted red-haired guy with eyes of a fox. I had seen him a couple of times when I was sweeping near his cell. But I did not know he was an ice cold murderer who would not hesitate to use his gun if he thought it necessary. He was indicted to also have had a hand in the gunning of O'Bannion. The judge had refused to have him bailed out. Therefore his gang mates had tried to get him out by bombing the wall.

I finally got a letter from the notary of Cap, who also was a lawyer. Mr. Nichols wrote me he was taking measures to bail me out. With a sigh of utter relief I sank down on my bed. Cap had not left me in the lurch. I would be thankful to him all my life. A friend in need is a friend indeed. The bail money was to be one thousand dollars. When, after I was released, I should make my get away, for instance to Canada, Cap would lose his money.

But after I got free I had to await my deportation. That the immigration authorities had put me in jail was no matter; it was the consequence of my own acts and it was far from me to blame the American people. If any country might be my second fatherland, then it sure would be the U.S.A., a country I had learned to love. I did not regret ever to have come here. If there was any country I felt at ease, it sure was the U.S.A. I had always found work, and all Americans I had had to do with had been good friends to me.

Next day I was summoned to the office where I was told my detention had ended and that I was set free on bail. I had to keep myself at the disposal of the authorities who would expel me in due time. Judgment had been passed over me; I had to leave the country. As soon as I received notice, I had to report to the immigration office.

The Lennox family had received information from the Yellow Cab Company about my detention. They were not told, however, where I was, and they had assured Hugh that I should be free soon. My custody had lasted five days though, so they had been very much worried about what might have happened to me. I came home in the morning. Hugh was not there, but Mary and Jeanie were. They weeped with joy by seeing me again. They were awful happy and Jeanie tenderly kissed me. Never before in my life had I been so glad to come home. The domestic sphere of the Lennox home appeared to me more pleasant than I could remember it did ever before. I thought even in my parental home in Holland I wasn't more at ease. But this was obviously due to my detention and the depressive surroundings in the Cook County Jail, the evil stench of which still pursued me.

I pondered about home with my parents where I always had had a snug and busy life. I blamed myself I had not written home for a long time and I neither had received any letters, probably because they did not know my address. I hoped all was well. Anyway, I should know about it soon enough, for it would not be long before my deportation was to be carried out. In the meantime I'd use the opportunity to enjoy life in the time that was left to me as much as I could. I had met with so much misery recently that I sure needed compensation some way or other. With a sigh of utter relief I sank into the easy chair in which I was always seated and looked at the bustle of the two women. Jimmy was still at school. It won't last long before I had to go, I thought. Then I had to leave all those dear people. I had accepted my fate and I sure wouldn't get my tail down. I'd like to step out with Jeanie as long as I could. Jeanie was more refined than her parents and she had her claims as to the way of being taken out. If she went with me, she mostly tried to go to the better places. Not that she made any difference in the intercourse with her parents because they had another pattern of thinking and living than we youngsters. She had very happy ties with her parents. As a matter of fact, she was unsophisticated and when we were out we had a really good time.

The day following upon my release from jail I went to the office of the Yellow Cab to get my back pay, for I had to quit my job because of the uncertainty pending my deportation. I had to keep myself at the disposal of the authorities and was not allowed to leave Chicago. I could not get to work very well on account of this. They all had been very nice to me and my fellow drivers were really sorry for the way I had to leave them. As a last treat to me Mr. McLean, the manager, offered me an invitation for attending the festivities held by the company on the occasion of the twenty-fifth anniversary of the president of the board, Mr. Charles Gray. The feast was to be held two days later on a Saturday evening in one of the halls behind the office. I went there with Jeanie. We hooked in on the polonaise and later we danced the newest dance—the Charleston. And we had a lot of fun. Early in the evening Mr. Gray himself together with his wife came to the feast and we all lustily sang: "Here comes Charlie, Here comes Charlie, Here comes Charlie, Here comes Charlie, Here comes Charlie, Here comes Charlie Gray!" The wall of the big hall resounded from the thumping of the dancers and of the band music. We came home late in the night. We slept out the following Sunday morning and in the afternoon we went to the beach for a swim.

I took my time to wander all over town to see the things I had not been able to. I climbed the steps of the El, bought fares, and drove with it miles and miles over the endless tracks, looking down upon the shops and the dark offices. I drove over the Lake Street viaduct, beneath which I had driven my cab so many times, till I got fed up with it. It looked to me a web of steel girders covering the dark traffic underneath; the trains nearly touched the windows of the buildings alongside. Rapid transit they called the El, which took you to the outlying points of Chicago. And the snug stations above the tracks over which the trains pounded gave something familiar to this old city railway.

I went down to State and Madison streets, the busiest street corner I ever saw. I walked twice the distance of the "Magnificent Mile" and roamed about Grant Park. The white

Wrigley building was light flooded at night, which gave a magnificent scene. Jeanie and I went shopping at Fields and later we went to the Midway Park and sat down at the new "Fountain of Time" monument. With deep draughts I enjoyed living my life the time left to me.

On September 26, 1926, I got the message to report myself at 2:00 P.M. at the office of immigration. From there they would take me to LaSalle Street Station to board the train to New York. In New York I should have to report to Ellis Island, where I should be lodged pending my departure by ship. The Dutch consul general had supplied me with a legal passport in order to ensure my departure. From him I learned that the American authorities had promised to grant me the necessary citizen's papers right away if I might choose to come back to the U.S.A. within a year, just because of my good record.

Next afternoon I said good-bye to Hugh, Mary, Jeanie, and Jimmy and to all I had gotten to know and made friends with. With a sad heart I took leave of this terrific city, a city I had gotten to love and where I had earned a good living. If you are away from Chicago you long back for it; the Loop, for State Street, the Wacker Drive, Michigan Boulevard, the big stations, the Soldier Stadium, the Lake, Dearborn Street and so on. Good-bye Chicago, good-bye friendly, boisterous, criminal, windy city. I shall miss you!

The train tickets were prepaid by the authorities, so I just travelled as a common train passenger in a sleeping compartment with four beds, two on each side above one another. There were already three people sitting in the compartment, a sergeant of the army and two civilians. When the train departed my three fellow passengers decided to play a game of poker. They lacked a fourth hand and therefore asked me to join. I had played cards in Holland, but I never played poker. But all the same I consented. At first I had to get used to their way of playing, but soon I got along quite well, although I did it my way. At 7:00 P.M. the Negro attendant came to make our beds and told us we "could gonna' sleep if we wanna' to." But we kept on playing cards until about 11:00 P.M. and then we went to bed. The train shaked that much I could not get asleep, so I just lied down thinking about what was going to happen to me in the near future.

The train trip lasted all night and we arrived at the New York Central Station at about 9:00 A.M. that morning. I had to report to the station master, who in turn informed the immigration authorities about my arrival. They took me to Ellis Island where I got a sleeping place in the big ward. There were more emigrants waiting for deportation. Everything looked very trim and neat and we were at liberty to do whatever we wanted except get away. In this respect we were deprived of our liberty. I got acquainted with a couple of Englishmen, who, like I, had jumped ship and also were expelled. With a number of other guys of other nationalities, we formed a sort of football team and played a soccer-competition. And so we had a good time for all that. We had at least a week to keep ourselves busy, for they had told me I was to be returned to Holland by the steam "Veendam" of the Holland-America Line.

September 30, 1926. I hear the yell of the boatswain, "Leggo"! The "Veendam" casts off its hawsers. I'm on my way from New York port back home.

Good-bye Cap and Sue, Lowell and Glenn, Good-bye Lyn, Dorothy, Jeanie. Goodbye to all who were dear to me.

Good-bye Manhattan!